# The Roman Empire

## DAVID WHITEHALL

Hodder & Stoughton

LONDON SYDNEY AUCKLAND TORONTO

## ACKNOWLEDGEMENTS

The publishers wish to thank the following for their permission to use copyright illustrations:
Aerofilms p14;
J Allan Cash Photo Library p17 right, 53 top right;
The Ancient Art & Architecture Collection p21 top left and right, 26 left, 33 bottom, 39, 44 top, 54 bottom right, 56 right, 57 right, 62 right;
Barnabys Picture Library p63 bottom right;
Bath Archaeological Trust p34 bottom right;
Biblioteca Apostolica Vaticana p50;
Birmingham City Council Library Services p4, 28;
The Bridgeman Art Library – Musée Crozatier, Le Puy en Velay p27 bottom right, – Cotton Nero Div. 25v p63 left;
Butser Archaeological Farm p13;
Reproduced by Courtesy of the Trustees of the British Museum p31 right (all);
C M Dixon p3, 15 top left, 19 top right, 36;
Ronald Embleton p45;
English Heritage p12, 55 bottom left;
English Heritage/Stephen Ellaway/Corbridge Museum p25 right;
Mary Evans Picture Library p33 top;
Sonia Halliday Photographs p22 top, 35 right, 41, 43 bottom, 53 to left;
Robert Harding Picture Library p55 right;
Michael Holford p55 top left;
The Kobal Collection p23, 27, 38 left, 52;
Erich Lessing/Magnum p22 bottom, 56 left;
The Mansell Collection p10, 19, 57 left;
Museo Nazionale Romano p30 top;
Museum of London p47 top;
National Trust p15 bottom;
Scala p5, 15 top right, 35 left, 48 bottom, 54 left, 62 top left, 63 top right;
St. Albans Museum Service p16;

Cover picture – Leicestershire Museums, Arts and Records Service.

The cover illustration shows a nineteenth-century painting of a Roman triumphal procession.

For Lucy, and Thérèse as always

**British Library Cataloguing in Publication Data**
Whitehall, David
 The Roman Empire. – (Past historic).
 1. Roman Empire
 I. Title  II. Series
 937.06

ISBN 0-340 54829 0

First published 1991

© 1991 David Whitehall

Illustrations by Joseph McEwan

All rights reserved. No part of this publication may be reproduced or transmitted in any form or by any means, electronic or mechanical, including photocopy, recording, or any information storage and retrieval system, without permission in writing from the publisher or under licence from the Copyright Licensing Agency Limited. Further details of such licences (for reprographic reproduction) may be obtained from the Copyright Licensing Agency Limited, of 90 Tottenham Court Road, London W1P 9HE.

Typeset by Litho Link Limited, Welshpool, Powys, Wales.
Printed in Hong Kong for the educational publishing division of Hodder and Stoughton Ltd, Mill Road, Dunton Green, Sevenoaks, Kent by Colorcraft Ltd.

# CONTENTS

| 1 | The Roman Republic | 4 |
| --- | --- | --- |
| 2 | Rome: From City to Empire | 6 |
| 3 | Rome and Carthage: From Rivalry to War | 8 |
| 4 | The Roman Villa | 12 |
| 5 | Roman Towns | 16 |
| 6 | Roman Roads | 20 |
| 7 | Games, Shows and Circuses | 22 |
| 8 | The Republican Army | 24 |
| 9 | Julius Caesar | 26 |
| 10 | The Emperor Augustus (27 BC–AD 14) | 30 |
| 11 | Religion | 32 |
| 12 | Family Life | 34 |
| 13 | The Roman Invasion of Britain (AD 43) | 36 |
| 14 | Emperor Nero (AD 54–68) | 38 |
| 15 | The Siege of Masada (AD 73) | 40 |
| 16 | Water for the People | 42 |
| 17 | Rome and its Provinces | 46 |
| 18 | Slavery | 48 |
| 19 | Christianity and the Emperor Constantine | 50 |
| 20 | Roman Architecture | 52 |
| 21 | The Latin Language and its Influence | 56 |
| 22 | The Empire's Decline and Fall | 58 |
| 23 | Change and Continuity | 62 |
|  | Glossary | 64 |
|  | Index | 65 |

Highlighted words are explained in the glossary on page 64.

# THE ROMAN REPUBLIC

For over 600 years huge areas of Europe, Asia and North Africa were part of a great empire. At its centre was the city of Rome.

From the Scottish borders to the Sahara Desert; in countries as far apart as Spain in the West and Syria in the East, people obeyed Roman laws. Yet, in 500 BC, Rome was just one of several small cities in Italy.

Until 510 BC Rome was ruled by kings. However, the rich families who lived there wanted power for themselves so they got rid of the king and made Rome into a republic. The king's power was shared between two men called consuls. However, to make sure they did not become too powerful, they were only allowed to rule for a year.

**A** This is a nineteenth-century painting of the Roman Senate.

For Romans who were not members of the Senate there was an Assembly. Here members were asked by the consuls to agree to new taxes and laws. Only `citizens` could take part – people who had the right to vote. People had to own land or property before they could vote in the Assembly. This excluded thousands of the poorest Romans. They had no say in the way the Republic was governed.

Before making any important decisions, consuls had to consult the Senate. This had about 300 members. These were the patricians, or leaders, of the richest families in Rome.

Together the consuls and the Senate formed an *oligarchy*. This is a term used by historians to describe a situation where a few people have all the power.

There were two classes of citizen – the patricians and the `plebeians`. For years the plebeians argued for an equal share in government. Finally, in 494 BC, they were allowed to elect two representatives called tribunes.

4

The tribunes attended every meeting of the Senate. They had the power to stop any decision they thought unfair.

In time the old differences between patricians and plebeians disappeared. In 200 BC laws which had stopped patrician men marrying plebeian women were ended. Many plebeians were becoming wealthy, not just from owning land as the patricians had done, but also from trade and business.

The patricians could not keep power to themselves. Eventually they allowed plebeians to become members of the Senate. Much had changed, but, as before, the richest families had most power.

> Today we work out our yearly dates from the supposed date that Christ was born. Before Christ (BC), the years are counted backwards. For example, Rome was ruled by kings until 510 BC. A year later it was 509 BC and Rome was a republic. From the birth of Christ dates are counted forwards. AD means *Anno Domini* ('in the year of the Lord').

**B** This source describes the funeral of a patrician man. It was written by the Greek writer Polybius in about 150 BC.

Before the dead man is buried they make a mask of his face. Then, during the funeral, a grown up son or some other relative makes a speech. In it he describes the dead man's achievements. After the burial they put the mask in the house where everyone can see it.

When any other member of the family dies they take the masks to the funeral. Here, they put the masks on men whom they most closely resemble. When the relative has finished speaking about the dead man, he describes the achievements of all the rest. They are present at the funeral in the form of their masks. In this way people find out about men who did good service to their country.

**C** Cicero, a Roman writer, wrote this account in about 50 BC.

Today, you can still read speeches in praise of people who died long ago. The families concerned keep them as a mark of honour. They use them if anyone else of the same family dies. The speeches keep alive the memories of the family's achievements. Of course, there is much in them which never happened. People invent successes and falsely claim their family were patricians.

**D** The Romans believed their city was built by twin brothers – Romulus and Remus. According to the story, their mother abandoned them when they were babies. They were rescued by a wolf who nursed them until they grew up. Eventually Romulus became King of Rome. With his brother Remus, he chose a site for the new city. It was near the place where the wolf had found them.

This is a copy of a bronze statue made around 500 BC.

1. Write out these dates in the correct order, starting with the earliest:
491 BC, 509 BC, 510 BC, 640 BC, 200 BC.
2. a) Discuss with a partner the meaning of the words: 'oligarchy' and 'republic'.
   b) Write out your definitions of these words.
3. a) What do you think is happening in source A?
   b) What information would the artist need to paint this picture?
4. a) Read source B. What is the attitude of Polybius to the funeral speeches and masks of the Romans?
   b) Compare source B with source C. Do you think Cicero agrees with the views of Polybius or not? Give reasons for your answer.
   c) What problems do these speeches give to historians studying Roman history?
5. Look at source D. Do you think this statue proves that the story of Romulus and Remus is true, or not? Explain why you think this.

# 2 ROME: FROM CITY TO EMPIRE

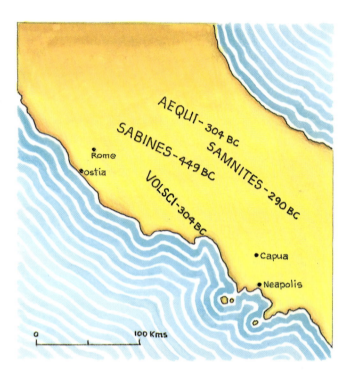

**A** This map shows where Italian tribes lived and the year each was defeated by the Romans.

In the early years of the Republic, the Romans were constantly at war. In 500 BC they were surrounded by many tribes. These were different groups of people, each ruled by their own chief. However, eventually the Romans ruled them all.

Firstly the Romans had to deal with the Sabines. Their home was in the mountain valleys north of Rome. They were defeated in 449 BC. The Aequi lived in the mountains of central Italy. By 304 BC, the Romans had conquered both them and the Volsci.

Once a tribe had been beaten, the Romans took half their land or more. They gave it to groups of army officers and soldiers. With their families these men formed colonies on the new lands. They were far from Rome but ready to fight when ordered.

Better treatment was given to those tribes which agreed to become Roman allies . They were allowed to keep their lands but had to pay taxes to Rome. In addition, all tribes had to contribute soldiers to the Roman army. The more tribes that were defeated, the bigger the army became.

With such a large army there was always the temptation to use it. By 220 BC the Romans ruled almost the whole of Italy.

They made some of the tribespeople citizens. This gave them certain rights: they were protected by Roman laws and they could vote at the Assembly. Furthermore, the most important jobs in the Republic were open to citizens.

A citizen could one day be a consul or command a legion in the army. He could live in Rome, now a very rich city, where he could marry into a Roman family and start a business or trade.

These were the benefits of being a citizen. It was a prize the Romans held out to tribes which made peace.

The only tribe still to be conquered was the Gauls. They lived in the Alps, mountains to the north of Italy. They had attacked Rome in 390 BC and burnt part of the city to the ground. It was the worst set back the Romans had suffered. Few of their historians wrote about it. Those who did concentrated on the bravery of the Roman soldiers.

**B** This account of the Gauls' attack is taken from the book, *Ancient Rome*, by Duncan Taylor (1960).

The Gauls clambered quietly up the path to the Capitol . A Roman sentry was supposed to be on guard there, but that moonlit night he did not do his duty. It was some white geese that gave the alarm. Their cackling woke Marcus Manlius. He threw the Gauls back as they struggled forward. Later, the Roman sentry who should have been on duty, was thrown after them.

**C** This account of the Gauls' attack was written by Livy, a Roman historian, in about 30 BC.

Rome was in very great danger. The Gauls had noticed there was an easy way up the cliff wall. So, on a starlit night, they first sent forward an unarmed man to try the way. Then, handing up their weapons where it was steep, they pulled one another up.

They reached the top in such silence that not only the sentries but even the dogs were not aroused. But the geese were! This saved them all, for the geese woke Marcus Manlius, a great soldier. He grabbed his weapons, and, at the same time, shouted to the others. He strode past his comrades to a Gaul who had a foothold at the top of the cliff.

With one blow of his shield, Manlius sent the Gaul tumbling, along with those next to him. The others let go of their weapons in fright. They tried to cling onto the rocks but were killed by Manlius. By now, the rest were hurling javelins and stones at the invaders. Soon all the Gauls lost their footing and were flung to their deaths.

Historians have to check the date of any source. Writers often describe events which took place long before they were born. Their accounts are called *secondary sources*. *Primary sources* are made by people who were alive at the time of the events.

A secondary source may have been copied from earlier primary sources. Ideally we would want to know where Livy got his information from. Some writers are more careful than others in the way they use evidence. The older the sources are, the more difficult it is to find out where the original information came from.

**D** This source is taken from *The Early History of Rome*, again written by Livy about 30 BC.
I wish to record for all time the story of the greatest nation on earth. I hope my writing has not been affected by my strong feelings about Rome's past. But I honestly believe that no country has ever been greater than ours, or richer in good citizens or brave deeds.

1 For each source in this section write down whether it is a primary, or a secondary source. Explain how you decided.
2 Read source D. Explain why Livy may be an unreliable source of information about Roman history.
3 Compare source B with source C. What differences do you notice between these two accounts of the Gauls' attack?
4 a) Look at source E. Does it support Livy's account, or the account written by Duncan Taylor? Explain your answer.
b) What additional information do you learn about the Gauls' attack from this picture?
c) Livy wrote his account during the Republic. Henri Motte painted his picture 1900 years later. Does this mean it must be less reliable than Livy's account? Explain why you think this.

**E** This is a modern copy of a nineteenth-century painting by Henri Motte.

# 3 ROME AND CARTHAGE: FROM RIVALRY TO WAR

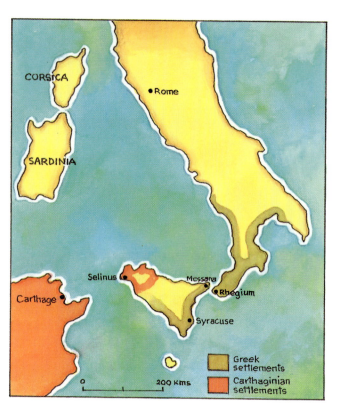

**A** This map shows Rome and Carthage in 270 BC.

Rome's most powerful rival was Carthage. This was a city on the north coast of Africa. Its people had grown extremely rich from overseas trade, and, like the Romans, they had an empire.

For a time there was peace between the two cities. Roman leaders agreed they would not interfere in areas ruled by Carthage. In return, Carthage's leaders promised to keep out of Italy.

However, this agreement did not last. In 264 BC Carthage and Rome fought the first of the three Punic Wars. Their struggle went on for a hundred years.

Without permission from their leaders, Roman mercenaries called Mamertines had captured the city of Messana. From here they had raided towns belonging to the Greeks and Carthaginians.

The Mamertines were heavily outnumbered by the Carthaginian army. So they appealed to Rome for help. Six years before, in 270 BC, Roman mercenaries had captured Rhegium. This was a city on the southern tip of Italy. The people here, unlike those in Messana, were allies of Rome. They had to be protected.

At Rhegium, the Roman soldiers had stormed the city walls, captured 300 mercenaries and executed them. Now, would Roman leaders treat the Mamertines in the same way, or would they help them?

The Romans argued in the Senate about what to do. Their decision led directly to the Punic Wars.

Four thousand Roman soldiers sailed to Messana. Carthaginian leaders thought the Romans had broken their promise. Over the years they had watched Rome conquer most of Italy. Messana might be the first step in their attempt to capture Sicily.

At that time the Carthaginian navy controlled the sea. However, on land the Roman army was a match for anyone and so the Greek colonists were quickly defeated. Despite this, it took another twenty-four years to beat the Carthaginians. The Romans had to win a series of battles on land – and at sea.

The First Punic War was over. The Second was soon to begin.

> Historians explain events like the Punic Wars by studying what caused them – the events that led up to them. They also study people's motives – the reasons why people behaved in the way they did.

**B** This account was written by Polybius in about 150 BC.
The Romans saw that the Carthaginians had brought not only Africa but also large parts of Spain under their rule. If the Carthaginians took control of Sicily, they would surround Italy and threaten every part of the country. It seemed clear that this would happen to Sicily unless help was given to the Mamertines. The Romans thought it was vital that they should not abandon Messana, otherwise the Carthaginians would use it as a base from which to invade Italy.

**C** This account is taken from *Rome against Carthage* by T A Dorey and D R Dudley (1971).
Roman leaders appealed to people's financial interests. They talked about the profits to be won from a war in Sicily. But it is likely they deliberately exaggerated. Roman leaders wanted to bring about war to boost their own military glory.

**D** In 260 BC one of the first sea battles took place between the Romans and the Carthaginians. Polybius describes what happened.

The Carthaginians eagerly put to sea with their fleet of 130 ships. They steered straight for the enemy and thought they could risk an attack without keeping any formation. It was as if they were seizing a prize which was theirs for the taking. As they neared the enemy, they saw the 'ravens' hoisted high above the bows of several ships.

At first the Carthaginians did not know what to make of these devices. They were completely strange to them. However, the leading ships attacked. But, as they rammed the Romans, they found that their ships were held fast by the ravens. Roman troops rushed aboard them by means of gangways which they let down. They fought hand to hand on deck.

Some of the Carthaginians were cut down. Others were thrown into total confusion and surrendered. The fighting seemed to have changed into a battle on dry land.

The rest of the Carthaginian fleet relied on their speed and circled round the enemy. They hoped they could safely ram them either broadside or from the stern. But the Romans swung their gangways round to meet an attack from any direction. Then they dropped the ravens so that any ship which came close could not get away.

At last the Carthaginians turned and fled. Because of these new tactics, they had lost their nerve. In all fifty of their ships were sunk.

1 Look at the map in source A and read source B. According to Polybius why did Roman leaders agree to help the Mamertines?

2 a) Look at the following list of causes and motives behind the First Punic War and then list them in order of importance:
(i) Roman leaders feared that Carthage would invade Italy from Sicily;
(ii) Four thousand Roman soldiers were sent to Messana;
(iii) Carthaginian leaders thought that Rome wanted to capture Sicily;
(iv) From Messana Roman mercenaries attacked Carthaginian towns in Sicily;
(v) Roman mercenaries captured Messana.
b) Do you think the causes or the motives best explain why the war started? Give reasons for your answer.

3 Read source C. What other motives did Roman leaders have for wanting a war?

4 a) Read source D. Where do you think Polybius got his information from?
b) Write down three facts which Polybius gives about this battle.
c) Now list any opinions which Polybius gives about the battle.
d) Is a historian's job made easier or more difficult when writers in the past give their opinions about people or events? Explain why you think this.

**E** This picture by a modern artist shows two ships: a Carthaginian quinquireme and a Roman trireme.

# HANNIBAL – ENEMY OF ROME

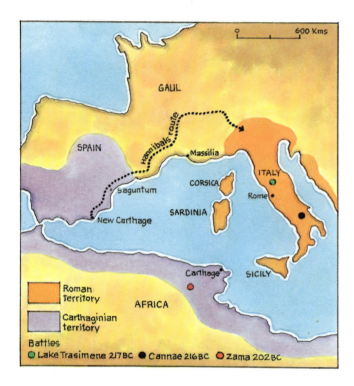

**A** This map shows Hannibal's route and the battles of the Second Punic War.

The argument which started the First Punic War was about Sicily. At the end of it the Carthaginians were forced to leave the island and pay a huge fine to the Romans. What they had not expected was to be told to get out of Sardinia and Corsica too. Hannibal, their new leader, wanted revenge.

It was impossible to attack by sea – the Roman navy was too powerful. However, Carthage still ruled much of Spain. From here Hannibal planned to invade Italy by land. But first he attacked Saguntum – a town in southern Spain allied to Rome. This meant war.

In May 218 BC Hannibal led an army of 90,000 footsoldiers and 12,000 cavalry out of New Carthage. Chained together at the back were thirty-seven elephants. With their earthshaking charge, Hannibal hoped that they would soon be trampling through lines of Roman soldiers. Ahead, was a journey of over 3,000 kilometres.

Twelve thousand soldiers stayed in Spain to guard the northern border. By October, the rest of the army had reached the Alps – the highest mountain range in Europe. Here it was constantly attacked by Gaullish tribes. Many soldiers had deserted or been killed on the journey. Hannibal's army was down to 23,000 men. Yet this army fought the Romans for the next ten years. It won a series of amazing victories.

For the Romans, each battle – Trebbia, Lake Trasimene and Cannae – was more disastrous than the one before. There was a real risk that Italian tribes allied to Rome would change sides and join Hannibal. Thousands of tribespeople had already done so and by 214 BC Hannibal ruled most of southern Italy.

> 1 At this point imagine you are leading the Roman army. Discuss with a partner what you should do next. Should you:
> (i) Bring all your forces together for a final battle against Hannibal?
> (ii) Invade Carthage?
> (iii) Keep a safe distance from Hannibal's army but attack groups of soldiers sent out to look for supplies?
> (iv) Make peace?
> (v) Invade Spain?
> Write out the order you would give and explain your reasons for it.

Throughout the War, Rome's allies stayed loyal. They sent their best soldiers to fight Hannibal. In 207 BC the Romans won a great victory at the Metaurus river.

Three years later, their army, led by Scipio, invaded Carthage. Hannibal had to follow and in 202 BC he was finally defeated at the Battle of Zama.

In 146 BC the Romans won the Third, and last, Punic War. This time Carthage was completely destroyed.

**B** This is part of a sculpture from a temple in Rome, built in the first century AD.

**E** During the Second Punic War, Rome ruled most of Sicily. In some towns their garrisons were attacked by townspeople loyal to the Carthaginians. In this source, written about 30 BC, Livy describes what happened in the town of Henna.

The citizens of Henna had arranged with Himlico, [leader of Carthage's Sicilian army] to betray the garrison. They decided that the keys of the town gate should be given to them.

Pinarius, the garrison leader, called his troops together and said, 'If we give up the keys, Henna will immediately be in Carthaginian hands and we will be butchered where we stand. Tomorrow, I shall be at the Assembly. By talking and arguing with them I shall keep things going. But when I give the signal, you are to hurl yourselves upon them. They will be unarmed and off their guard.'

Next day soldiers took their positions. Pinarius came out before the people and one or two called out, 'Give up the keys.' Soon everyone was shouting this. When it was clear they were on the point of violence, Pinarius gave the signal. His men rushed down upon the mob, while others stood at the gates to bar the way out.

The people of Henna were penned in and cut down. Panic increased the confusion: the victims, desperate to escape, came tearing down over each other's heads. The heap of bodies rose higher and higher. Pinarius said the Sicilians would now stop betraying the Roman garrisons. In fact, the story of the massacre was all over the island in a single day and many towns now joined Carthage.

**C** This is a modern artist's impression showing some of the dangers Hannibal's army faced while crossing the Alps.

Historians study the results, or consequences, of past events. Some consequences are more important than others.

**D** This source was written by Appian, a Greek historian, in about 150 BC. In it, he describes some of the consequences of the Punic Wars.

The Romans gave out the lands they had won to anyone who was willing to work them. They did this in order to increase the number of Italian people who owned land. But the very opposite happened. The rich took most of these lands. Next to them were the allotments of their poorer neighbours. They persuaded some, and forced others, to sell their land.

As a result, [the Romans] came to own huge areas of land instead of single estates, and used slaves to work them. Thus certain powerful men became very rich, the number of slaves increased throughout Italy, and Italian people were unemployed.

2 What information do you learn about Roman warships from source B?

3 Look at source C. Explain what difficulties Hannibal's army had in crossing the Alps.

4 a) Read source E. Do you think Pinarius was right to order the massacre at Henna? Give reasons.
b) What, according to Livy, was the consequence of the massacre?

5 a) These are some of the consequences of the Punic Wars:
i) The Romans destroyed the city of Carthage;
ii) Carthage had to give its land in Spain to Rome;
iii) Scipio became very famous;
iv) Carthage was no longer Rome's rival;
v) In the future there was nothing to stop Rome building up a huge empire.
Read source D. Add to this list other consequences of the war that are mentioned by Livy.
b) Work with a partner. Copy out the whole list. Give a mark out of ten to show how important you think each consequence was.
c) Do you think the job of a Roman leader would be easier or more difficult after the Punic Wars? Explain why you think this.

# 4 THE ROMAN VILLA

The Romans were determined to make good use of the land they had won. They therefore gave it out to army officers and government officials. These were people the Romans could trust.

As they needed homes to live in, one of the first things the new owner did was to build a villa. A villa might be a big house in the country with a huge farming estate attached to it. Other villas were built near towns.

Many tribes lived in circular, wooden huts. Most Roman villas were made from brick and stone and were rectangular in shape. This meant that other rooms could easily be built onto them.

> For this reason there is no such thing as a typical Roman villa. They were all different. Each one was built to a separate design and many were extended over the years.

Most villas were working farms. They provided crops for sale at the town market nearby. Many larger villages were worked by slaves. In Gaul and Italy especially, they produced wine and olive oil for export throughout the Empire.

The actual day-to-day running of the villa might be left to an `overseer`. He was employed by the owner. Part of his job was to supervise the slaves. They lived, chained together, in a separate part of the villa.

For some owners slavery was not the best way to grow crops. They thought they would get better work if they paid local people to farm their estates. Generally, if they could grow more crops, villa owners would make bigger profits. This would also help Roman traders in the towns. Farm workers now had wages to buy the goods that they sold.

Some villa owners were willing to `lease` part of their land to local people who could then grow their own crops and pay a rent in return. At first the rent was in goods – gifts of cattle and food. Later, rents were paid in money.

Local people could employ workers of their own. Soon they were free to sell their crops and buy land. With their profits they too built villas. The first were often no more than rectangular huts.

**A** This is an artist's impression of the Roman villa at Lullingstone.

**B** Many tribespeople lived in huts. These are reconstructions of huts at Butser Farm in Hampshire.

Later they extended them using Roman building materials – tiles and wall plaster, with concrete for the floors. In some parts of the Empire these materials were not available or were too expensive. Here, people made do with timber walls, but there was a difference. Now the walls had foundations, just like the Roman villas.

These villas were important. They showed that people across the Empire were beginning to accept a new and different way of life. They were beginning to live like Romans.

**C** This source was written by Columella, a Roman writer in about AD 60. He offers advice to villa owners with large estates.

My advice at the start is to appoint an overseer. You should choose a man who has been hardened by farmwork since childhood. He should be middle-aged and physically strong. He should be skilled at different types of farm work. He must be willing to learn new jobs. It does not matter if he cannot read or write. If he can remember things, he will be able to manage things well enough. He must take care of the equipment and iron tools.

The overseer is also in charge of the slaves' clothes. The clothes should be useful, rather than smart, and keep out the wind, cold and rain. Leather tunics, patchwork clothes and hooded cloaks are best. The overseer should be strict but fair. He must never be cruel and should have a sense of humour.

1  a) Work in groups. Compare source A with source B. Discuss how the homes are different. Write down five of the most important differences you have noticed.
   b) Do you think it would be light or dark inside the villa? Give at least two reasons for your answer.
2  The following sentences may be true or false. Write out any true ones and correct any false ones:
   (i) Roman villas were all built to the same design.
   (ii) All Roman villas were made from brick and stone.
   (iii) Most villas were working farms.
   (iv) All Roman villas were worked by slaves.
   (v) Roman villas were only built in the country.
3  Read source C. You own a villa and need an overseer to run your estate. You intend to interview several men for the job. What questions would you ask them?

# ROMAN VILLAS – PROBLEMS WITH THE EVIDENCE

In many parts of Europe, it is still possible to tell where a villa once stood. Villa sites show up on aerial photographs. Sometimes the remains of walls can be seen. This is because the soil above them is darker in colour.

However, once the soil has been removed, little evidence may remain of the actual villa. Bricks and tiles could have been taken from it. These would have been used by local people for their own buildings.

Some materials survive better in soil than others. For example, it is unusual to discover the remains of wood, cloth and leather, yet all of these items would help to build up a better picture of the Roman villa.

Today, much of our information about villas is based on nineteenth century archaeological evidence. At that time archaeologists concentrated on rooms lived in by the owner's family. They discovered the remains of bathrooms, and found mosaics set into the floor. These were hundreds of coloured tiles, pieced together to form a pattern or picture.

From this evidence, historians explained how luxurious life must have been on a villa. This was really all they were concerned with. However, their explanation was misleading. Not all villas were like this. But for years people knew little else about them.

Archaeologists and historians had less interest in other parts of the villa. They spent little time excavating stables, barns and the buildings where estate workers and slaves lived. As a result, they knew far less about these people's lives.

Historians now know that townspeople relied on the villas to provide food. They did not have to grow their own. This meant they had more time to set up trades in the town.

So villas were important to many people, not just those who owned them. Without this evidence, past historians did not realise how important villas really were.

> Historians can provide different explanations of the past. A lack of evidence may be one reason why they sometimes disagree.

**A** This photograph clearly shows the rectangular shaped rooms of a villa in Radnorshire.

**B** A mosaic from Tabarka in Tunisia. It shows a villa surrounded by fruit trees.

**C** The rooms in some villas were heated by hypocausts. This picture shows a hypocaust from the Roman Villa at Chedworth. Heat from a furnace would circulate under the floor. The room would also be warmed by hot air rising through flues (stone pipes) in the walls.

**D** This is a wall painting from a villa in Pompeii.

1. Look at source A. Suggest two reasons why there might not be much archaeological evidence left of this villa.
2. Study sources B, C and D. What idea do you get of Roman villas from these sources?
3. Make a list of ten things in your home which archaeologists might find a thousand years from now. Next to each one explain what they would learn from it.

# 5 ROMAN TOWNS

**A** This is an artist's impression of the forum at St Albans.

The Romans built towns throughout the Empire. They were not a new idea. Years before the Romans, the Egyptians and Greeks had lived in towns.

The Romans copied their example. The difference was that Roman towns were usually much bigger. They also built far more of them.

There was a reason for this. In towns the Romans could keep a close eye on the people they had conquered. In Britain they moved tribes down from the hills into new towns like St Albans.

The Romans built shops, and provided fresh water supplies and proper drainage. These were the benefits of life under the Romans.

They also set up councils of local people to run the towns and collect taxes. The Romans encouraged tribal leaders to become members. In return, the Romans allowed them to keep their lands: the tribal leaders would be an example to others. Soon they would think and behave like Romans.

A town in Britain was similar to one in any other part of the Empire. First, the Romans chose their site. Then surveyors marked a line around it. This was for the walls.

Next, they mapped out straight lines for the streets. These crossed each other at right angles. Between them were the blocks of land which the Romans would build on.

In any Roman town the most important building was the *basilica*. This was a law court and assembly hall. The *curia*, or council office, was nearby. In front of the basilica was the *forum*.

This was the market place. Here people could buy fruit and vegetables from farmers' stalls. They could also find out the latest news and listen to orators. It was the centre of the town and always busy.

16

Most towns had a temple where people could pray to their gods. They could spend their free time at the theatre. Larger towns had public baths.

The bigger a town was, the more public buildings it had. These would be added over the years. The Romans used different materials to build them. In the first ones they used wood and stone. Later on, they could build from concrete, brick and marble.

Some towns increased in size, filling all the blocks up to the town walls. Others did not. So Roman towns were not exactly the same. Each one went through changes at different times.

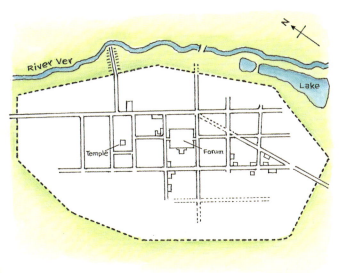

**B** A town plan of St Albans based on archaeological evidence.

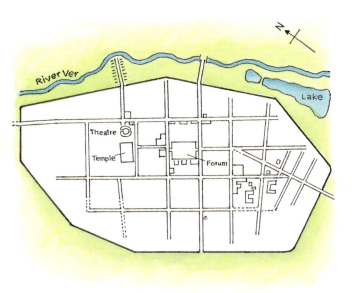

**C** A fourth-century plan of St Albans based on archaeological evidence.

**D** This source was written by Tacitus, a Roman historian, in the first century AD.

Through towns the Britons became used to peace and a relaxing life. The Romans helped them to build temples, squares and houses. They led the people into the pleasures of banquets and baths. But these novelties were only proof of their slavery.

**E** This photograph shows an excavation at a Roman site, Maiden Castle in Dorset. An archaeological site is divided up into numbered areas. Each part of the site is drawn and photographed. Notes are made about it. Evidence is carefully collected and numbered according to the area it was found in. Various tools are used including small trowels and brushes.

1. Read the text and source D. Why did the Romans build towns?
2. Look at source A. The artist has drawn his picture from archaeological evidence. Work with a partner. From the picture, list the archaeological evidence which you think would survive today.
3. a) Compare source B with source C. Do you think source B shows a street plan earlier or later than the one in source C? Explain your answer.
   b) What changes took place in St Albans? Suggest reasons for these changes.
   c) From source B suggest two reasons for the siting of St Albans.

## OUT IN THE STREETS

The streets were busy from early in the morning. People got up at dawn and were soon out shopping. Bakers had been at work long before then, grinding flour and making bread.

Along the streets shopkeepers took down the wooden shutters from their shop fronts. Overnight they had padlocked them to hooks in the pavement. It was the best way of protecting their shops. They did not have a door or glass front. They served people from a counter which opened out onto the street.

There were no supermarkets. Each shop sold a particular item. Most streets had a butcher, a bakery and shops which sold fruit and vegetables. There were always food shops nearby. These sold hot snacks or drinks from clay containers sunk in the counter.

However, shopkeepers faced competition from street traders. These people walked up and down the streets selling anything from hot sausages to salt. They had to avoid barbers who shaved their customers in the middle of the pavement.

The best shops were around the forum. Here, people could buy goods imported from all parts of the Empire. There were many jewellers, together with shops selling pottery and glass ornaments. Some goods would be made by a skilled craftmaker in the back of the shop.

This area might also be the worker's home. Or they might live with their family in a single room above the shop. They might not get much sleep at night as carts clattered through the streets. The drivers had no choice – by law only funeral carriages and chariots on special occasions could travel through a town during the day. The rest had to wait outside the town gates. This kept the streets free for shoppers and pedestrians.

The streets were noisy. They could also be dirty. Not all Roman towns had drains. Instead they had a drainage channel down the middle of the street. This carried rubbish and waste water from the shops. In heavy rain it would overflow, making the road muddy and slippery to walk across.

Stepping stones were the answer. These were put down where streets crossed. They were far enough apart to allow carriage wheels through, but close enough for shoppers to step onto.

**A** This is a modern artist's impression of a Roman street.

**B** This sculpture shows women working in a shop. Sometimes women owned shops and became rich from their trade.

**C** This account was written by Cicero in about 50 BC. In it, he gives his opinion about some of the trades that were carried out in Roman towns.

Some types of work are suitable for a gentleman. The common trades are not. A gentleman should not do a job that is done by hired workmen. These men are unskilled and we pay them simply to work with their hands. The job of a workshop mechanic is also unsuitable. They are all involved in common trades.

Least respectable of all are fishmongers, butchers and cooks. You can add to this list, the makers of perfume and dancers. But there are jobs which require a high level of intelligence and everyone benefits from them. Medicine and architecture, for example – and teaching. These are proper jobs for a gentleman. But of all the ways to earn a living, agriculture is the best. There is nothing more suitable for a gentleman.

**D** The interior of a Roman food shop from the third century AD.

**E** Few Roman writers described the towns they lived in. This account written by Juvenal describes what it was like to live in Rome during the first century AD.

Many a sick man dies here from lack of sleep. How can anyone sleep in rented lodgings here? Only the rich get any sleep. There is the noise of carts trundling through the narrow streets. And the shouts of their drivers when they get stuck would wake even the heaviest sleeper.

In the streets, however fast we hurry, there is always a huge crowd ahead and people behind us pushing and shoving. You get dug in the ribs by someone's elbow. Then someone hits you with a long pole, another with a wine jar. My legs are sticky with mud. Before long I am trodden on all sides by large feet and a soldier's boot sticks into my toe.

At night, tiles can fall from roofs and brain you. People throw their broken pots from the windows above. You shouldn't go out without making a will. And there is only the moon, or the faint light of a candle to help you home.

1. Compare source A with a busy street in a modern town. Work with a partner and list as many differences as you can between the two. Then make a second list and write down any similarities you can think of.
2. a) Read source E. What problems does this writer mention about life in Rome?
   b) How useful is this source to historians who want to find out about life in a British town?
3. What type of shop is shown in source B?
4. a) Read source C. What was Cicero's attitude to the work shown in source B?
   b) Do you think everyone in Roman times agreed with his views on work, or not? Explain why you think this.

# 6 ROMAN ROADS

Throughout the Roman Empire, towns and provinces were linked together by roads. At first, they were built for the army. Their main purpose was to move troops and supplies quickly. Some of these roads covered huge distances. They were better than anything that had been built before.

Surveyors marked out a new road using stakes. They checked these were straight using an instrument called a groma. This was important. A straight road meant shorter travelling times.

However, roads had to change direction to avoid some obstacles and zigzagged uphill. But, if a road had to cross rivers or marshland, it could often be kept straight. Roman engineers were skilled at building wide bridges.

Skilled workmen were needed to build roads: quarrymen, carpenters and stonemasons. The heaviest work was done by slaves. They were supervised by army engineers.

The first of these great roads was the Appian Way. It was finished in 312 BC and connected Rome with the southern port of Brindisi. Eventually, this road, like many others, was improved, and new ones were built.

Better roads led to more trade. Crops could be moved more easily from the country to the towns. So could raw materials from the provinces. These were needed by local craftspeople to make goods for sale across the Empire.

In Roman times people travelled a great deal. They walked, or rode on donkeys or on horseback. Merchants carried their goods on wagons or carts.

A  A Roman road being built.

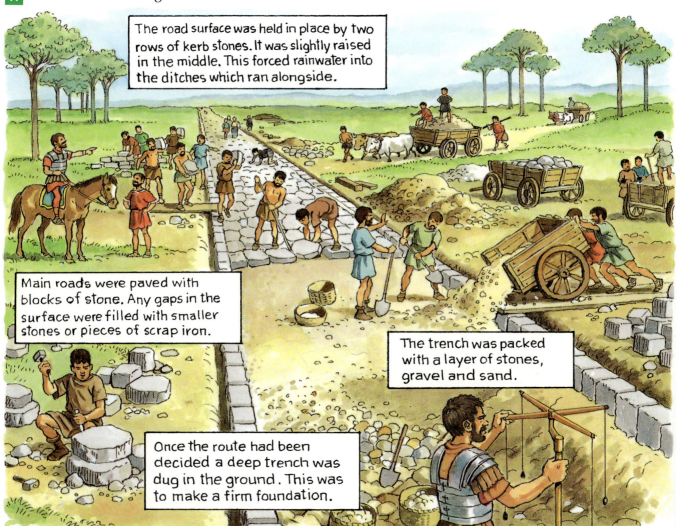

**B** Roman carriages are shown on stone carvings. From this evidence, nineteenth century historians decided that the carriages were uncomfortable and difficult to steer.

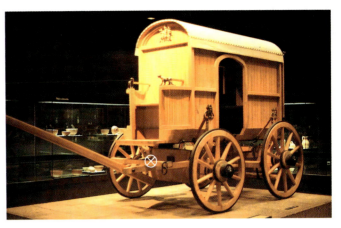

**C** This is a reconstruction of a Roman carriage. It is based on archaeological evidence found in Germany in 1983. The front axle turned on a pivot (X). This made steering easier. Suspension gave a more comfortable ride.

Archaeologists can provide new evidence about the past. Because of it, historians sometimes have to change their previous explanations.

**D** This map shows the main roads of the Roman empire in the second century AD.

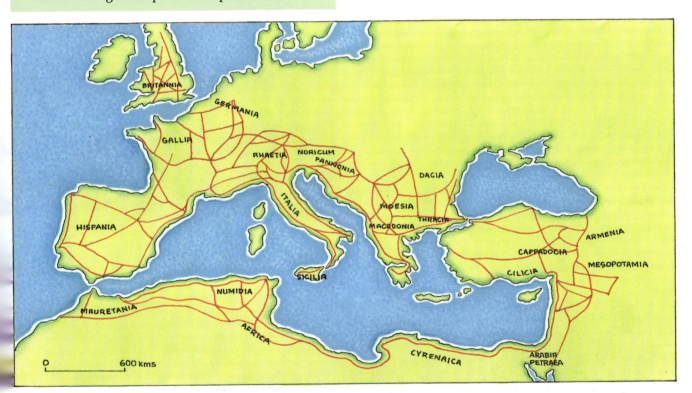

1. Look at the various jobs being done in source A. Copy the list of workers given below and, next to each one, briefly describe the job they did: stone mason; surveyor; slave.
2. a) How does source B disagree with source C?
   b) Why did nineteenth century historians believe that Roman carriages were uncomfortable and difficult to steer?
3. a) Does source C prove:
   (i) All carriages were like this?
   (ii) Stone carvings are not reliable evidence?
   (iii) Some carriages were uncomfortable?
   Explain your decision.
4. a) Look at source D. Use an atlas. Which modern countries were part of the Roman Empire?
   b) How do the sites of Roman roads compare with modern ones?

# 7 GAMES, SHOWS AND CIRCUSES

For Romans who wanted entertainment, a town was the place to be. At street corners there were travelling performers of every sort. People could watch conjurors and clowns, jugglers and snake charmers.

Many towns had theatres where Greek and Roman plays were performed. The largest open air theatres could hold 10,000 people. Smaller theatres held music competitions and poetry readings. They were rarely full.

Much more popular were the chariot races which took place in the circus . The biggest was the Circus Maximus in Rome. On public holidays 250,000 people would cram into it to watch the races.

The chariots raced wheel to wheel and crashes were common. When this happened the charioteers had to cut themselves free of the reins. They had to do it quickly, otherwise they would be trampled to death by the horses behind.

The Emperor went to the races in Rome. Sometimes he ordered purses filled with gold to be thrown to the crowd. Or he gave out raffle tickets with marvellous prizes. Jewels, villas and even ships could be won. It was another way to keep the people of Rome happy.

More popular still were the shows which took place in the amphitheatre . Here, gladiators fought to the death. Most of them were criminals or slaves captured in war.

Different gladiators carried different weapons. Thracians fought with a small circular shield and dagger. A retiarius carried a net and trident .

Roared on by the crowd, the fight began. People watched with increasing excitement as the gladiators wounded each other. They cheered when one of them was killed. Attendants made sure the victim was dead by striking his forehead with a mallet.

**A** This fourth-century mosaic shows a wild animal fight in the amphitheatre.

**B** This mosaic of a chariot race was made in the third century AD.

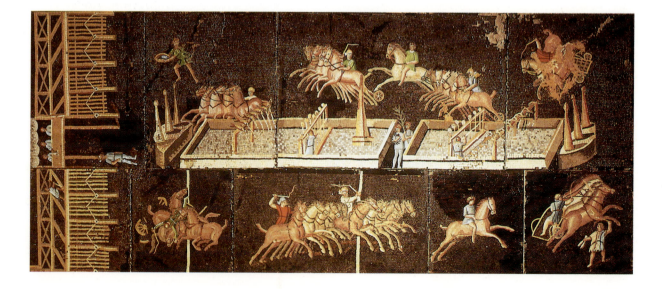

**C** This photograph is from the 1956 film *Ben Hur*.

Some sources provide more information than others. They can also give a different view of things from other sources. This is true of pictures, as well as written sources.

**D** This is an extract from *Daily Life in Ancient Rome*, by Jerome Carcopino (1941).
In Rome there were 150,000 unemployed people. About the same number finished their work at midday. The shows occupied the time of these people. They kept their attention. People who are bored are ready to revolt. All the emperors competed with each other to add extra shows. Some of these started at sunrise! Through them, the emperors could keep order in Rome. This meant that the Empire would be safe.

**E** This source is taken from Cicero's *'Letters to Friends'*, written in 55 BC.
If you ask me, the games were magnificent. The wild beast hunts, two a day for five days – magnificent, there is no denying it. But what pleasure is there in seeing a puny human being mangled by a powerful animal? Or watching a splendid beast run through with a hunting spear?

1. a) Look at source B. Is it a primary, or a secondary source? Give reasons for your answer.
   b) Describe as fully as you can, what information it provides about Roman chariot racing. To help you, look for: an official throwing water on the chariot wheels; officials showing the number of laps; an official encouraging the horses with a whip.
   c) What do you think was the job of the single horsemen in the race?
   d) What evidence suggests that chariot racing was dangerous?

2. a) Look at source C. Is this a primary, or a secondary source? Explain why you think this.
   b) Use this source to describe five sounds you would expect to hear at a chariot race.
   c) What additional information about chariot racing do you learn from source C that is not shown in source B?
   d) Do you think these sources give different impressions about chariot racing? Give reasons for your answer.
   e) Which source provides the most information about chariot racing? Explain why you think this.
   f) Does this mean that the other source is useless as evidence? Give reasons for your answer.

3. Read source D and source E. Explain how the emperors' attitude to the games was different from Cicero's.

# 8 THE REPUBLICAN ARMY

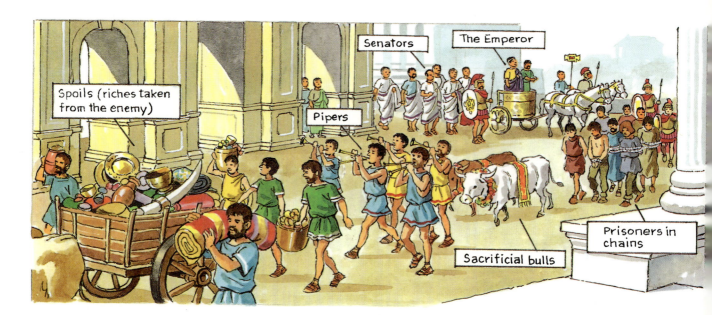

**A** This picture is by a modern artist. It shows the triumph of Emperor Trajan after his victory in the Dacian Wars. It is based on stone carvings from Trajan's Column, built in AD 113.

When Rome first became a republic in 510 BC it had one legion to defend itself. This was an army of about 4000 men. Only citizens could join the army, and they had to own property worth over 400 denarii.

The men were unpaid volunteers who fought with their own weapons and armour. They swore an oath to obey the consul who led them in battle. Discipline was strict. Legionaries who failed to obey orders risked severe punishment. Deserters were executed.

During the wars against the Italian tribes, the legion was increased to 6000 men. Defeated tribes had to send auxiliaries for the army. Therefore, as Roman leaders gave citizenship to people throughout Italy, thousands of men could be called on to fight.

The army's job had changed. Not only could it defend Rome, but it could win new lands by attacking Rome's enemies.

At first legionaries were part-time soldiers. Many of them were farmers who left their land in the spring and summer. This was when most wars were fought. It was also the farmers' busiest time.

Farmers had crops to harvest and sell. Wars that went on longer meant that farmers got into debt. They sold their farms and joined the army full-time.

In 300 BC Rome had four legions. Each one was led by a general chosen by the Senate. They obeyed the orders of the consul. In the Second Punic War (218–201 BC) Rome fought Hannibal's army with twenty legions.

Each year more citizens were needed to replace those who had been killed, but there were fewer and fewer volunteers. The Senate's solution was to conscript men – force them to join whether they wanted to or not.

In 107 BC the consul Marius opened up the army to all citizens. He got rid of the law requiring legionaries to own property. Now, thousands of poorer Roman citizens joined the army, hoping to make their fortune.

*After 396 BC legionaries were paid and provided with weapons – an oval shield, a short sword and a javelin.*

In addition, Marius made legionaries carry their own food and equipment. Previously this had been carried on carts dragged by mules or donkeys. This had slowed the army down.

Steadily, the consuls and Senate lost control over the army. By 100 BC it had become too big – sixty legions spread across the Empire, hundreds, even thousands of miles from Rome. Legionaries took an oath to obey the general who commanded them. Previously, this oath had been to the consuls – the elected leaders of the Republic.

*Generals were chosen by the army and had great freedom. Those who were successful could guarantee their legionaries riches in war.*

This new oath put the Republic in danger. Generals who disagreed with decisions made by the Senate had the power to stop them. They could use their legions as private armies – and this is what happened.

For long periods between 100 and 30 BC rival generals fought each other in a series of civil wars. The Senate and the consuls could not stop them. The army, which had been set up to protect the Republic, now brought it to an end.

> Historians study changes in the past. They try to discover why these happened. Sometimes changes cause other changes to happen.

**B** In the early twelfth century, Zonarus wrote this account of a Roman triumph. He based his account on a source written in about AD 200 by the Greek historian Dio Cassius.

A general had to win a great success before he was worthy of a triumph. Then he was immediately given the title Imperator by his soldiers. On arriving home, he would ask the Senate if he could hold a triumph. If the Senate agreed, he kept his title of *Imperator*. Wearing his uniform and a crown of laurel leaves, he called his troops together.

After praising them, he presented them with money and medals. He gave out gold and silver coins to each man with their name on it. After these ceremonies, the triumphant general rode in his chariot through the city. At the head of the procession were the spoils – everything that had been taken during the war. Then he gave out a large part of the spoils to the soldiers who had taken part. But some generals distributed them amongst all the people. If anything was left over, they would spend it on temples or some other public building.

**C** This model of a Roman legionary is based on archaeological evidence found at Corbridge, Northumberland.

> 1 a) Match the list of statements below with their correct dates:
>   (i) Legionaries were provided with weapons.
>   (ii) The army was made up of sixty legions.
>   (iii) Rome had one legion to defend itself.
>   (iv) Rome fought the Second Punic War with twenty legions.
>   (v) The Roman army had four legions.
>   (vi) Men did not have to own property to join the army.
>   Dates: 510 BC, 396 BC, 107 BC, 300 BC, 100 BC, 218 BC.
>   b) Show this information on a timeline.
> 2 a) Answer the following questions:
>   (i) Why did the Roman army increase in size?
>   (ii) Why were soldiers paid?
>   (iii) Why was conscription introduced?
>   b) Write down three other ways in which the Roman army changed. For instance, explain what other change it brought about.

# 9 JULIUS CAESAR

**A** A statue of Julius Caesar.

In 60 BC the three most powerful men in Rome were Gnaeus Pompey, Marcus Crassus and Julius Caesar. They were famous for the wars they had won. Pompey had brought large parts of Asia, Syria and Judea under Roman control.

Crassus was a respected general. He had put down a revolt by thousands of Roman slaves. Soon Caesar would conquer Gaul and invade Britain. These three men ruled the Empire under an agreement called the First Triumverate. It did not last.

Crassus was killed in 53 BC. This left Pompey and Caesar as chief rivals for power. The Republic had always been ruled by two consuls. Now the Senate ordered there should be only one – Pompey.

Caesar was due to return to Rome from Gaul in 49 BC. Here he had been provincial governor. The big question was: would he disband his army and accept Pompey's rule – or would he fight?

Without his army to protect him, Caesar feared that Pompey would have him killed. So, in January 49 BC he led his troops across the Rubicon River. This was the border between Gaul and Italy. Once he crossed it, war was certain.

Caesar chased Pompey's army to Greece. In 48 BC Caesar defeated his army at the Battle of Pharsalia. Pompey escaped to Egypt where he was eventually betrayed and murdered.

This did not end the fighting. Caesar led his army in Asia Minor, North Africa and Spain, beating his enemies each time. By 45 BC the Roman Empire was under his total control.

Caesar made the laws. He kept the Senate and the People's Assembly but reduced all their powers. The Republic was over.

He formed colonies throughout the Empire and rebuilt many public buildings. He also introduced the Julian calendar. This changed the number of days in a year from 355 to 365.

In Rome, Caesar halved the number of unemployed people entitled to free corn. Instead he tried to create jobs for them outside the city.

The main problem Caesar faced was to let people in the Empire know about these great changes. Today, leaders use newspapers, television and radio to get their messages across. The Romans used coins.

On each coin there was an inscription. It was usually abbreviated so the coins could carry a lot of information. Whatever was printed had to be approved by the Roman leader. Caesar was no exception. His coins told people what he wanted them to know. Caesar was bald, but he made sure that coins and statues did not show this.

**B** A Roman coin of 44 BC. It shows Julius Caesar on one side. On the other is Juno, goddess of women.

Historians describe information controlled in this way as 'propaganda'. The information can be unreliable, so historians always check their sources. They need to ask *who* made the source: who wrote the letter? or who painted the picture? Once a historian knows this he or she can ask *why* the source was made. These questions are important. They might explain why a source gives only part of the truth.

**C** The Greek writer Dio Cassius wrote this account in about AD 200.
The Senate gave Caesar the title 'Father of his Country'. They had this stamped on coins. They said his birthday should be marked by public sacrifices. In addition, they ordered that a statue of him should be set up in all the cities and in the temples of Rome. This was because they were enjoying peace as a result of Caesar's efforts.

**D** This account of Caesar was written by Suetonius, a Roman writer, about AD 110.
In the Senate Caesar either met with no opposition or threatened anyone who dared to interrupt. Marcus Cato once tried to delay the work of the Senate. He talked for hours in a debate. Caesar had him forcibly removed and led off to prison.

Lucius Lucullus went too far in opposing Caesar's plans. Caesar so terrified him with threats that Lucullus fell on his knees and begged Caesar's pardon. Caesar lost no opportunity to pick quarrels, however unfair and dangerous.

**E** This photograph shows an actor appearing as Julius Caesar in a film.

**F** This nineteenth-century painting shows a chief of the Gauls about to surrender to Caesar. Caesar is at the red table.

**G** This account was also written by Suetonius.
Caesar was a most skilful swordsman and horseman. If he reached a wide river he would either swim or float across it on an inflatable skin. In battle, if the fight was a hard one, he used to send the horses away – his own first. This was a warning to men who were frightened. They could not hope to escape on horseback. If Caesar's troops gave ground he would encourage them. He would catch individuals by the throat and force them round to face the enemy again.

1. Which of the sources do you think are propaganda? Give reasons for your choice(s).
2. a) Look at source B. Why do you think Roman leaders had their faces printed on coins?
   b) Why might Caesar choose the goddess Juno for the reverse side of this coin?
3. a) What impression do you get of Caesar from source C?
   b) Do you think Caesar would have approved or disapproved of this impression? Explain your answer.
4. a) Read source D and source G. What information do you think Suetonius would not have been able to publish in Caesar's day? Give reasons for your answer.
   b) What information in these sources would Caesar use as propaganda?
5. Use any of the sources in this chapter to design your own coin to show the achievements of Julius Caesar.

# THE MURDER OF CAESAR (44 BC)

**A** This is a nineteenth-century painting of the death of Julius Caesar.

Not all of Caesar's decisions were popular. But for two years no one dared to argue. He made the laws. At any time he could order a huge army to crush his opponents.

Caesar behaved like a king. He ignored the wishes of the Senate, the tribunes and the People's Assembly. Under the Republic people had shared power. Now it seemed those days had gone for good.

Caesar brought peace to Rome and the rest of the Empire. Some people were jealous of his success. Others hated the  dictatorship  he had set up. Amongst them were Brutus and Cassius, two of Caesar's friends. In secret, they plotted to kill him.

They planned the murder for the 15th March. On that day Caesar had called a meeting of the Senate.

> Historians do not know for certain what happened next. The sources do not agree. Historians have to compare the sources and piece together all the information they give.

**B** This account was written by Suetonius in about AD 110.

As soon as Caesar took his seat, the  conspirators  crowded around him. Tilius Climber came up close, pretending to ask a question. Caesar waved him away but Climber caught hold of his shoulders. 'This is violence!' Caesar cried.

As he turned away, one of the Casca brothers stabbed him with his dagger just below the throat. Caesar grasped Casca's arm and ran it through with his knife. He was leaping away when another dagger blow stopped him. With drawn daggers all around him, [Caesar] pulled his toga over his face. As he stood there he was stabbed with twenty-three dagger thrusts.

Caesar did not say a word after Casca's blow. Even so, some people say that when Brutus was about to stab him, Caesar said 'You too my child?' Members of the Senate escaped in confusion.

Caesar was left lying dead for some time. Then three slave boys carried him home in a  litter , with one arm hanging over the side.

**C** This account was written by Plutarch, a Roman writer, about AD 90.

Tilius Climber took hold of Caesar's toga and pulled it down from his neck. This was the signal for the attack. Casca struck the first blow in his neck. Caesar turned round, seized the dagger and held it fast. The others closed in on Caesar in a circle.

Whichever way he turned he was hit with blows. Knives were aimed at his face and eyes. He was driven like a wild beast. Some people say that he fought them all, dodging this way and that. But when he saw that Brutus had drawn his dagger, he pulled his toga down over his head and sank against the base of Pompey's statue. The statue was drenched with his blood.

They say he received twenty-three wounds. Many of the conspirators were wounded by one another as they directed so many blows against one body.

D Suetonius wrote this account of Caesar's funeral, in about AD 110.

Caesar's coffin was carried to the Forum by magistrates

Two men set fire to it with blazing torches. At once the crowds of by-standers heaped upon it dry branches and whatever else they could find. Then the musicians and actors tore off their robes. They had taken these from the equipment of Caesar's triumphs and threw them into the flames.

Soldiers threw in their weapons. Many of the women too, offered up their jewellery and the robes of their children. There was much sadness, and crowds of foreigners were crying. Saddest of all were the Jews who flocked to the place for several nights in a row.

After the funeral, people with torches in their hands ran to the houses of Brutus and Cassius. They were forced back but killed a man called Helvius Cinna by mistake. They thought he was Cornelius Cinna, who had bitterly criticised Caesar the day before.

They put his head on a spear and paraded it around the streets. Afterwards the Romans set up a marble column in the Forum almost twenty feet high. On it they inscribed the words 'To the Father of his Country'.

At the foot of this column people continued for a long time to sacrifice and make vows. They settled their disputes by an oath in the name of Caesar.

In his will, Caesar named Mark Antony as the next Roman leader. But he gave most of his fortune to Octavian, his great-nephew. Together they defeated Caesar's murderers at the Battle of Philippi in 42 BC. Unfortunately, like Pompey and Caesar before them, Mark Antony and Octavian became rivals. They divided the Empire between them – Antony took the eastern half, Octavian the west.

Their rivalry led to war. It ended in 31 BC with Octavian's victory at the Battle of Actaeum. Mark Antony committed suicide soon after. Octavian was the new Roman leader. He became more powerful than Caesar had ever been.

1. a) Work with a partner. Compare source B with source C. Write down ways in which their accounts of Caesar's murder are different.
   b) Explain why these sources might be unreliable.
2. Read the following statements and then write them down. Next to each, explain whether you think the statement is sensible or not. Remember to explain why you think this.
   (i) Source A is from a nineteenth-century painting so it provides no useful information about Caesar's murder.
   (ii) Only one of the sources is correct. The others must be wrong.
   (iii) All the sources provide some useful information about Caesar's murder.
3. Read source D. Does this source prove that Caesar was a popular leader or not? Explain your answer.

E This is a modern artist's impression of Caesar's funeral.

29

# 10 THE EMPEROR AUGUSTUS (27 BC – AD 14)

**A** Augustus as chief priest. This sculpture is from the first century AD.

Julius Caesar ended the Republic. He had changed it into a state ruled by one man. Octavian made it an empire. In Roman history the word 'empire' has two meanings. It describes all the provinces ruled by a Roman leader. It is also the name for the type of government set up by Octavian.

He made himself *Imperator* (Emperor). After a victory in war, commanders were praised as *imperators* by their troops. Caesar had used the word as part of his name. So Octavian took it as well. He wanted Romans to remember that he was Caesar's nephew and adopted son. This was important. Soon after, the Senate made Caesar into a god.

Octavian was backed by sixty Roman legions. He could make whatever changes he wanted. So it was a surprise in 27 BC when Octavian offered to give up most of his powers.

It was just a show. The Roman people wanted peace and order. Only Octavian could provide it. The Senate returned all his powers but agreed to govern a few safe provinces. Octavian kept command of the armies in Spain, Gaul and the East. The Senate gave him a new title too, 'Augustus', meaning 'majesty'.

People could pretend that Rome was still a Republic and that everyone had a share in government. But there was a difference. All the important decisions were made by Augustus.

He started a public fire brigade in Rome, and a postal service in Italy. He got rid of pirates from the Mediterranean and built new roads across the Empire. It was a time of peace. Farmers, craftspeople and traders found it easier to sell their goods.

In AD 6 Augustus made Judea a province. His one real disaster came in AD 9. Augustus had hoped to extend the province of Gaul, moving its border from the River Rhine to the Elbe. In trying to do this, German tribes slaughtered three Roman legions. It was one of the worst defeats in the army's history.

In AD 14, shortly before he died, Augustus wrote a document listing all his achievements. He did not mention the Roman defeat in Gaul.

**B** Differences between the Roman Republic and Empire.

Laws were made by consuls who were advised by members of the Senate.

The two consuls took it in turns to lead the army.

**C** This extract is from a document written by Augustus just before he died in AD 14.

I fought many wars throughout the whole world by land and by sea. I spared the lives of all citizens who asked for mercy. I extended the frontiers of all the provinces of the Roman Empire. I brought peace to Gaul, Spain and Germany. I stopped the civil war. With everyone's agreement, I became all-powerful leader. Then I returned the state to the control of the Senate and the people of Rome.

**D** Brutus and Cassius were two of Caesar's murderers. Augustus defeated them in 42 BC at the Battle of Philippi. This source, written by Suetonius in about AD 110, describes what happened next.

He showed no mercy to his beaten enemies, but sent Brutus's head to Rome for throwing at the feet of Caesar's statue. He insulted the more distinguished of his prisoners. When one of them humbly asked for the right of a decent burial, he got the cold answer, 'That must be settled with the crows.' And when a father and his son pleaded for their lives, Augustus, it is said, told them to decide which of the two should be spared by drawing lots or playing a game. The father sacrificed his life for the son. He was executed; the son then committed suicide. Augustus watched them both die.

**E** Two sides of the same coin minted in 28 BC. The abbreviated words *CAESAR DIVIF* mean son of the divine Caesar. *LIBERTATIS* means freedom. On the reverse side of the coin *PAX* means peace.

The consuls carried out laws made by Augustus.

**F** This is the reverse side of a coin minted between 27-20 BC.

1. Match the events in List A with the correct dates in List B. Write them out in chronological order.

| List A | List B |
| --- | --- |
| Battle of Philippi. | 42 BC |
| Death of Augustus. | AD 14 |
| Senate gave Octavian the title Augustus. | AD 9 |
| Judea made a province. | 27 BC |
| Defeat of three Roman legions in Gaul. | AD 6 |

2. Look at source E. Why would Augustus remind people that he was the son of Caesar?

3. a) Look carefully at sources E and F. Explain what message you think Augustus is trying to put across.
   b) Which source supports the impression given by these coins? Explain why this might be.

4. a) Read source D. What impression do you get of Augustus from this source?
   b) Explain why this source might not be reliable.

Augustus led the army.

# 11 RELIGION

```
600  500  400  300  200  100        100  200  300  400  500  600
              BC                                AD
```

**A** In Rome religious ceremonies took place in the Forum. This modern artist's impression is based on a carving from the Arch of Marcus Aurelius, Rome (third century AD).

There were temples in most towns across the Empire. On special days priests held ceremonies to please the Roman gods. The most powerful god of all was Jupiter. He was chief of the Gods. There were many others including Minerva, the goddess of wisdom, and Vulcan, the fire god.

Roman temples were often quite small, so the most important ceremonies took place outside. Sometimes animals were sacrificed. Hundreds of people would watch as a calf or lamb was killed on the temple steps. They hoped the gods would help them in return.

People prayed to spirits too. The Romans believed these were everywhere – in rocks, in birds, in grass and even in lightning.

It was believed that spirits could help people, or do harm. It depended on how they were treated. The Romans set up statues to the spirits and made offerings of bread and wine. This was to keep them happy.

Just as important as the temple priests were the augurs. They tried to find out the opinion of the gods on various matters. They looked for signs in the sky. These came from either thunder or the flight of birds. Augurs studied the `entrails` of sacrificed animals. From them, they explained what the future would hold.

Augurs and priests were elected by members of the Senate. Later on they were appointed by the emperor. In this way, Roman leaders could control what was preached. Throughout the Empire the message was always the same. The gods agreed with Roman government. Emperors could be gods too and everywhere people were encouraged to pray to them.

At certain times of the year there were religious `festivals`. These reminded Romans of their duty to obey the gods. Many festivals were public holidays. People enjoyed the wild animals' fights and chariot races which went with them.

The Romans were fairly `tolerant`. They allowed people in the provinces to follow their own religions. Some of these became popular with Roman soldiers. They helped to spread the worship of other gods from other parts of the Empire.

One of their favourites was Isis, an Egyptian goddess. Soon she was being worshipped in Rome. Mithras was another. He was a Persian god of truth and light. Each new province that the Romans conquered increased the number of gods they could worship.

However, there was one condition. These other religions must not interfere with people's duty to obey the Romans. This meant worshipping the emperor above all other gods.

The Jews and the Christians refused. They were cruelly treated by the Romans. Their rival religions had to be stamped out – but the Romans did not succeed.

**B** Livy wrote this account in about 30 BC.

> During the winter of 218–217 BC many strange things happened in Rome – or people said they had happened. Others believed them, though there was little evidence for the strange things they described. This is always the case with superstitious people.
>
> A six-month-old baby shouted 'victory' in the vegetable market. In the cattle market an ox had walked up three flights of stairs. Then, when the lodgers screamed, the ox was so frightened that it leapt out of the window. Shapes like shining ships had appeared in the sky. The Temple of Hope had been struck by lightning. At Lanuvium a spear had moved of its own accord.
>
> In Picenum it had rained stones. In Gaul a wolf had pulled a sentry's sword out of its sheath and run off with it. In Sicily some soldiers' javelins had burst into flames. At Praeneste it had rained red hot stones and at Arpi the sun fought against the moon. At Falerii the sky split and opened wide, while through the hole a great light shone.

**C** This bronze head of Minerva, the Roman goddess of wisdom, was discovered by workmen in Bath in 1727.

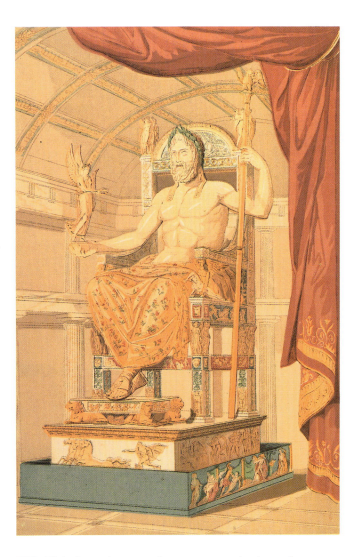

**D** This is a nineteenth-century painting of Jupiter, the chief of Roman gods.

1. The following sentences may be true or false. Write out any true ones and correct any ones that are false.
   (i) The Romans did not believe in spirits.
   (ii) The Romans continued to worship their old gods, but also followed new religions.
   (iii) Across the Empire people's religious beliefs changed because they had to worship the emperor.
   (iv) The Romans' religious beliefs did not change.
2. a) Read source B. What is Livy's attitude to the strange things he describes? Explain how you decided.
   b) Suggest explanations for these strange happenings.
   c) How would Roman priests explain them?
   d) What does this source tell you about the Romans?
3. a) Explain how Roman religion was different from religion in Britain today. Use all of the sources to help you.
   b) What similarities can you think of?

33

# 12 FAMILY LIFE

**A** A family scene from a wall painting at Pompeii.

The Romans considered the family a very important part of life. Happy family scenes are shown on many wall paintings and stone carvings. They showed how good Roman families should behave. The reality was sometimes quite different.

This is part of a letter which a Roman soldier wrote to his wife in 1 BC. 'If you give birth to a boy, keep it. If it's a girl expose it.' Under Roman law a father could kill his new born child. He might expose it – leave it to die of cold and hunger, perhaps to be eaten by dogs on a rubbish dump. Thousands of baby girls were killed in this way.

When a girl married, her father had to provide a dowry. This was money or gifts which would be given to the girl's husband. Many families could not afford it. For them it was easier to kill a girl when she was newly born.

During the Republic a father could sell his children into slavery. He was the *pater familias* – the head of the household. He had complete control over his wife and children. In effect, he owned them.

It was a serious crime for a woman to commit adultery. A man could sentence his wife to death. It was not until the time of the Empire that this law was changed. More often, unhappy marriages ended in divorce.

Women were not allowed to vote. The male Senate passed laws which treated them unfairly. They could not ride in carriages through the streets and their clothes had to be in plain colours.

These were laws that Roman women managed to stop. For three days they blocked the streets of Rome. Finally the Senate gave in and changed the laws.

Parents taught their children at home until they were about seven. Girls learnt from their mothers how to cook, clean and mend clothes. If they were lucky they learnt to read. Boys were taught by their fathers. People thought boys were more useful than girls. They could help their father at work and join the army.

At seven children were usually sent to school. This might be a room in the school teacher's house or in the back room of a shop on a town street. Here they learnt reading, writing and arithmetic. Lessons began at dawn but finished early in the afternoon. Discipline was strict. Pupils who were late might be beaten with a stick.

Girls left school when they were about twelve, but might carry on their lessons at home. At this age boys went to a secondary school. Here they learnt history, arithmetic and astronomy.

At home children played board games. They had toys like dolls and models. Most families had a pet – usually a dog or a cat. Historians know this because these animals were often carved on tombstones.

**B** Roman household objects.

34

Roman families usually ate three meals a day. They had breakfast of bread and fruit. For a midday lunch there was a light meal of vegetables, perhaps with meat or fish. Families ate their main meal at about 5 o'clock. It could go on for hours in the house of a rich family. For poorer people it was over much sooner. They had less to eat and less choice of foods.

**E** This mosaic shows two athletes, the winners of a local contest.

**F** This is an inscription from a tombstone made sometime between 135 and 120 BC.

> Stranger my message is short. Stand by and read it through. Here is the unlovely tomb of a lovely woman. Her parents called her Claudia. She loved her husband with her whole heart. She had two sons. She was cheerful in conversation and well-mannered. She kept the house. She made wool. That's my last word. Go your way.

**C** This wall painting shows guests being entertained after a meal.

Most written sources in Roman times were produced by men. They give us little information about women's lives. Sources sometimes have gaps which historians have to fill.

**D** This source was written by Pliny, a Roman writer, in about AD 100.

I was sailing in a boat on Lake Como when an older friend called my attention to a villa near the lake. 'From that room,' he said, 'a woman once threw herself and her husband.' I asked him why. He continued, 'Her husband was suffering from an ulcer in his private parts. His wife looked at it. No one else could give a more honest opinion of whether it was curable. She saw it and gave up hope. She tied herself to her husband and plunged with him into the lake.'

1  a) What impression do you get of the family in source A?
   b) Suggest reasons why this source might *not* give a true picture of Roman family life.

2  a) In pairs, look at the household objects in source B. Copy and complete this table. The first one is done for you.

| Type of object | Made from | Used for |
|---|---|---|
| Jug | Clay | Holding liquid |

   b) Do these objects suggest the Romans were very different from people today, or not? Give reasons for your answer.

3  Does source D suggest: (i) men were more important than women in Roman times; (ii) women were more important than men; (iii) both men and women were equally important? Explain your answer.

4  a) From reading this chapter, what impression do you get of Roman women?
   b) Do any of the sources give a different impression of Roman women? Explain why you think this.

# 13 THE ROMAN INVASION OF BRITAIN (AD 43)

**A** Historians have very little pictorial evidence about the invasion of Britain. They have to rely on sculptures of battles with Gaulish tribes. This carving is from a stone coffin in Rome.

Julius Caesar was the first Roman leader to invade Britain. He attacked in 54 BC and defeated the British tribes. Their chieftains signed a treaty, promising to pay taxes to the Romans.

Caesar sailed with his army back to Gaul. He never returned. Neither, for the next ninety years, did any other Roman leader. This all changed in AD 43.

Rome had a new emperor – Claudius. He wanted to invade Britain and make it part of the Empire. He ordered Plautius to organise an army of 50,000 men. Plautius was one of the few generals that Claudius could trust.

Plautius had problems. By the summer of AD 43 he had an army ready at Boulogne. But his men were refusing to move. They feared that Britain was at the end of the world. Eventually Plautius persuaded them to board the ships, but several weeks had been lost.

This was lucky for the Romans. British tribes had been waiting on the other side of the English Channel. Now it was late in the summer. They decided the Romans had left it too late to invade. They went back to their fields to gather in the harvest. They were wrong.

The army landed at Richborough in Kent. Here archaeologists have discovered the remains of a Roman fort. By building a fort, the legions could be protected from attack. It gave time to search the surrounding country for the enemy tribes.

The British tribes were led by two brothers – Caratacus and Togodumnus. They were chieftains of the Catuvellauni tribe. They had to move quickly. Their capital was at Camulodunum (Colchester). They thought the Romans would soon try to attack it.

Other British tribes joined the chieftains' army. It lined up on the banks of the River Medway, and waited.

**B** Mark Hassall, a modern historian wrote this extract in 1979.

Claudius was worried about his position as Emperor. He felt threatened by members of the patrician families in the Senate. They wanted Rome to return to the Republican form of government. If Claudius was to keep his throne he had to keep the loyalty of the army. He needed a successful campaign with plenty of booty for the soldiers. Claudius would then be allowed a splendid triumph in Rome.

E This source was written by Dio Cassius in about AD 200. He based his account on the reports of Roman army commanders. He describes what happened after the army reached the River Medway.

The barbarians thought that the Romans would not be able to cross without a bridge. So they lined up in a relaxed way on the other side. But Plautius sent across a small force of Germans. They were used to swimming easily in full armour. They totally surprised the enemy. But instead of fighting, they stabbed the horses used to pull the enemy's chariots.

Plautius then sent Vespasian and Sabinus across the river with their troops. They also took the enemy by surprise and killed many of them. The survivors did not flee, but fought again the next day.

It was not certain which side would win. Finally Gnaeus Geta, after narrowly avoiding capture, managed to soundly defeat the Britons. The enemy withdrew their troops to the River Thames. The Britons did this without problem. They knew where the firm ground was and where to cross.

However, the Germans swam across again. Some others got over by a bridge a little way upstream. Then they attacked the barbarians on all sides at once and cut down many of them. In chasing after the rest, they fell into swamps. It was difficult to get out and many Romans drowned.

Shortly after, the barbarian leader Togodumnus was killed. But instead of surrendering, the Britons fought even more fiercely than before. Because of this fact, and because of the difficulties he had faced crossing the Thames, Plautius became afraid.

He did not advance any further. Instead, he guarded what he had already won and sent for Claudius. Plautius had been told to do this in case he met with any fierce fighting. And in fact a lot of equipment, including elephants, had already been assembled for the expedition.

Claudius was in Rome. When the message reached him he set off for Britain. He took command of the legions which were waiting for him near the River Thames. He crossed the river and faced the barbarians. He defeated them in battle and captured Camulodunum. Then he won over many tribes.

C This is a modern artist's copy of a stone carving from the triumphal arch of Marcus Aurelius, third century AD.

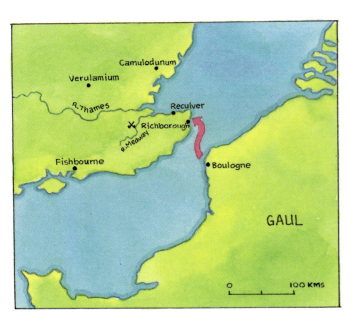

D This map shows the route of the Roman army in AD 43.

1 a) Look at source A. Do you think the Romans or the Gauls are shown on horseback? Explain your answer.
b) Which side had the better weapons and armour?

2 Source C shows a scene from a war fought by the Romans in the third century AD. Explain why it might be useful to a historian studying the Battle of Medway.

3 According to source B what motives did Claudius have for wanting to invade Britain?

4 a) Read source E. You are Plautius. Write to the Emperor. Describe the invasion in detail and explain why you need his help.
b) Source E suggests that Plautius stopped at the River Thames because he was frightened to continue. Suppose this was not the real reason at all. Can you think of any other reason why he stopped?
d) Why might Dio Cassius' evidence be unreliable?

5 Historians do not know for certain where the Battle of Medway took place. What evidence might help them find out?

# 14 EMPEROR NERO (AD 54-68)

**A** This source is taken from a film about Nero's life, *Quo Vadis*, made in 1951. It shows the Emperor playing a lyre while Rome burns in the background.

Claudius died in AD 54. He was poisoned by his fourth wife, Agrippina. His son Britannicus should have been the next emperor, but Agrippina wanted to rule the Empire with her son, Nero. The army agreed and Nero became emperor instead. He was seventeen years old.

In his first speech to the Senate, Nero promised to behave like Augustus. However, Nero had far less interest in ruling the Empire. He enjoyed poetry, ballet dancing and acting. These were very unusual hobbies for a Roman emperor.

According to one writer, no one could leave a theatre when Nero was acting. The gates were shut. Women gave birth in the audience. One man became so bored he pretended he was dead. Many people offered to carry him out for burial.

Nero executed anyone who criticised him, including his mother. He feared that Britannicus might one day be his rival. He therefore had him poisoned. He divorced his first wife, then ordered soldiers to strangle her. Poppae Sabina was his next wife. Nero kicked her to death.

Yet Nero did try to make some good changes. He made sure the unemployed in Rome were always well supplied with corn. He also wanted poorer people to pay less tax – but the Senate stopped him.

There was peace throughout the Empire. People were free to trade and make money. The inscriptions on Nero's coins described his achievements. But writers at the time did not explain them in any detail. Instead they concentrated on his crimes.

They accused him of setting fire to Rome in AD 64. Historians today do not know whether Nero was really to blame. Roman writers had no doubt.

The Senate eventually declared Nero a public enemy. He fled from Rome and committed suicide in June AD 68.

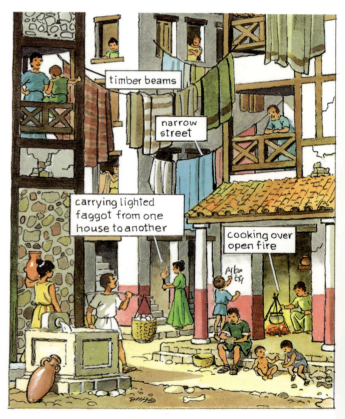

**B** Thousands of poor people lived in blocks of flats. There was always the risk of fire.

Historians' opinions of past events change through time. Modern historians may have a different opinion from past historians, so their explanations may also be different. Sometimes historians living in different places have different opinions.

**C** This account was written by Suetonius in about AD 130.

Nero was disgusted by the old buildings and the narrow streets of Rome. So he set fire to the city. A group of people caught some of Nero's men armed with tar and flaming torches, but they dared not interfere. The terror lasted six days and seven nights.

Nero watched the fire from the Tower of Maecenas. He was delighted by the beauty of the flames. Then he put on an actor's costume and started to sing. He offered to remove corpses and rubble free of charge. But he allowed nobody to search among the ruins. He wanted to collect as much loot for himself as possible.

**D** The Roman historian Tacitus wrote this account in about AD 120.

The fire started near the Circus Maximus. Here there were shops which sold inflammable goods. Instantly the fire took hold. It was driven by the wind and the whole circus was soon ablaze. Here the houses were not built of stone. There was nothing to stop the fire spreading through the narrow streets.

A number of men threatened anyone who tried to put it out. They threw burning sticks into the fire, shouting that they were obeying orders. Nero at this time was at Antium. He did not return to Rome until the fire approached his house. But it could not be stopped.

However Nero opened up many public buildings so the homeless had somewhere to stay. He brought supplies of food from Ostia and reduced the price of corn. But there was a rumour about Nero. People said that when the fire was at its height, he was acting and singing on a private stage.

After five days, the fire was put out. Meanwhile Nero took advantage of Rome's sorry position and built a palace for himself – the Golden House. He also rebuilt areas of Rome which had been destroyed. He made sure the streets were wide. He gave money so people could rebuild their houses or flats. Some people said these were useful changes and made Rome more beautiful. But nothing could stop people believing that Nero had ordered the fire.

**E** This source is from *Roman History from Coins*, written by Michael Grant (1958).

People usually forget that Nero achieved remarkable successes abroad. For years, Roman leaders had argued with the King of Parthia over the country of Armenia. But, in AD 66, Nero made an agreement with the King, and for the next fifty years there was peace.

It was the emperors' responsibility to make sure food supplies reached Rome and to give out free or cheap corn. Nero was determined to be generous and popular. In AD 64 he planned to leave Rome for a while, but the people stopped him. They hated the idea of his going.

After the fire of AD 64, Rome was replanned very wisely and, all the time, many people supported his government.

**F** A bust of Nero.

1  a) What impression do you get of Nero from source C?
   b) What evidence does Suetonius use to blame Nero for the fire?

2  a) Read source D. Look at this list of words: proud; ashamed; pleased; angry; disappointed.
   Write down any words which you think best describe Tacitus' attitude towards Nero. Give reasons for your choice.
   b) What evidence does Tacitus put forward to suggest that Nero was guilty of ordering the fire?
   c) Compare sources D and E. Which do you think gives the fairer picture of Nero? Give reasons for your choice.

3  a) What evidence in source C and source D suggests that Nero might *not* have been responsible for the fire?
   b) How does source B support the view that Nero might not have been to blame for the fire?

4  a) Read source E. What impression do you get of Nero from this source?
   b) Look again at the list of words in question 2. Why might this historian not have any of these feelings about Nero?
   c) Is it possible to believe that Nero was both cruel *and* successful? Explain why you think this.

# 15 THE SIEGE OF MASADA (AD 73)

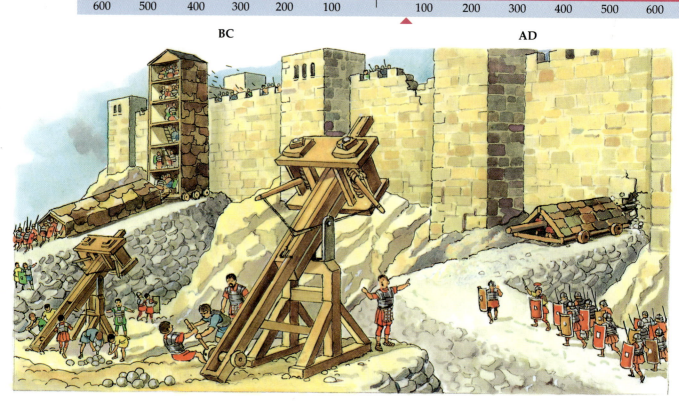

**A** This is an artist's impression of the Siege of Masada.

In Syria and Judea the Jews refused to accept Roman rule. Like the Christians they were `persecuted` because of their religion. They believed in one God, and would not pray to the emperors.

Jerusalem was a holy city. The Romans made it their capital of Judea. This was too much for the Jews and, in AD 66, they started a `revolt`.

The Jews won an incredible victory and forced the Roman army out of Jerusalem. Next year the Romans sent an even bigger army led by Vespasian. He had 50,000 men to try and win back the city. The fighting lasted four years.

Eventually Vespasian's son, Titus, recaptured Jerusalem. Over a million people had been killed or wounded. But this was not the end of the revolt. Jews still held out in the fortress of Masada.

> Some primary sources are eye witness accounts but some are not. In order to judge how much trust can be placed in a source, historians try to check where earlier writers have got their information from.

**B** What happened next is described in the following sources by Flavius Josephus. He was a Jewish historian who wrote in AD 75. He lived in Rome and was a friend of both Vespasian and Titus. He based his account on the battle reports of Roman generals.

The new Roman governor in Judea was Flavius Silva. He built a wall right round the fortress, so that none of the Jews could escape. The Romans had to bring supplies for the army from a great distance. Even drinking water had to be fetched as there were no springs in the area.

He had found only one place where it was possible to build platforms for his siege weapons. This was on a rock called the White Cliff. But it was 450 feet [140 metres] below Masada. Silva ordered his soldiers to pile earth onto it. Soon they had built a solid platform 300 feet [100 metres] high. On top of this platform they built a ramp made of huge stones fitted together. In addition, the Romans built a tower, covered all over with iron plates. The tower was for the `ballistas` and stone throwers. These [men] pelted the defenders on the walls and forced them to take cover.

Silva then ordered a great battering ram to be built. This swung repeatedly against the wall, until a small section collapsed. Inside, however, the Jews had built a second wall.

Seeing this, Silva ordered his men to hurl flaming torches against it. Soon the whole wall was ablaze. The Romans returned to their camp full of delight. At night they kept watch to see that no one escaped.

**C** In this source, Josephus, who wrote source B, describes what happened next.

Eleazar was leader of the Jews. That night he gathered them together and made this speech. He told them, 'It is clear that at daybreak our resistance will come to an end. We cannot defeat our enemies in battle. Let us die without becoming slaves to them.' [Eleazar was proposing mass suicide as a solution to their problems.]

Eleazar had many arguments to put forward, but his listeners stopped him. Full of enthusiasm, men rushed off to kill their families.

In the end not one man failed to carry out the deed. They made a huge heap of all their possessions and set fire to them. Then the men lay down beside their murdered wives and children.

Ten had been chosen by lots to be the executioners of the rest. They slaughtered them all by cutting their throats. There was one man left. He set fire to the fortress, then drove his sword through his own body.

These men died thinking that everyone had been killed. But two women and five little children survived. They had hidden in tunnels that carried water to the fortress from underground. Of the rest, 960 men, women and children were killed.

At dawn the Romans got their weapons ready. They expected further fighting. Seeing no enemy but a dreadful quiet on every side, they wondered what had happened. At last the Romans shouted. The two women heard and came out of the tunnel. They gave the Romans a detailed account of what had happened. They found it difficult to believe them. But then the Romans discovered the rows of dead bodies.

1 For each source write down whether it is a primary or a secondary source. Explain how you decided.

2 Read source B and look at source D. What problems did Flavius Silva have in laying siege to Masada?

3 a) Read source C. From whom did Josephus probably get his information?
b) Why might this account of Eleazar's speech be unreliable?
c) Read the caption to source B. For what other reason might Josephus' account of the siege of Masada be unreliable?

4 Work with a partner. You are Roman newspaper reporters. You have been asked to write a report about the siege of Masada. Think of a headline, and then, in your own words, explain what happened.

5 Source A shows siege machines being used to attack Masada. Study them in groups and describe how you think they worked. One person from each group should present their ideas to the class. How similar are your ideas?

**D** An aerial photograph of Masada showing: (1) palace; (2) baths; (3) storerooms; (4) palace; (5) swimming pool; (6) Snake Path Gate; (7) West Gate; (8) underground water reservoir ; (9) Roman siege wall; (10) Roman camps; (11) White Cliff.

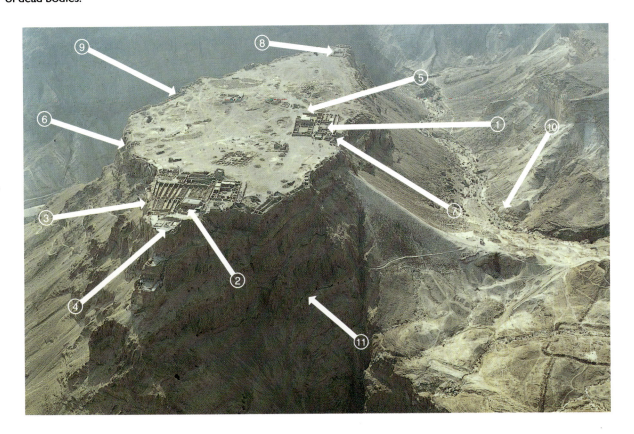

# 16 WATER FOR THE PEOPLE

The Romans took the problem of water supply very seriously. At first, rivers and wells provided the water they needed. But, as the population of towns increased, they were no longer enough. In Rome engineers came up with a solution. They built aqueducts.

The word 'aqueduct' has a simple meaning – to bring water. There was nothing simple about the constructions built to do it.

Rome had twelve aqueducts, bringing spring water from the hills round the city. One of the aqueducts – the Anio Novus – was 104 kilometres long. Each day the aqueducts supplied the city with over 1000 million litres of water.

The first aqueducts carried water underground in lead or earthenware pipes. However, they often broke under the pressure of water. So engineers built tunnels of stone or brick called conduits. These were about 1¼ metres wide and 1¾ metres high. They were lined with hard cement and had a roof of stone.

The Romans did not have machines to pump water all the way. So they built the conduits on a gentle slope. This presented a problem when valleys had to be crossed. They solved it by building the conduit on a continuous row of arches. Engineers had discovered that the arch shape could support great weights above it.

The piers and arches were made from stone-faced concrete. This was stone set in mortar on the outside with layers of concrete on the inside. To make the concrete, masons had first to lay stones on the area to be filled. Then they covered the stones with mortar to bind them together.

Water from the aqueducts was brought to a reservoir in the city. This had three tanks and pipes leading from it. The first supplied Rome's public gardens and fountains. The second carried water to the baths. The third supplied Rome's private houses. People paid a tax for it in return.

The Romans built aqueducts in various parts of the Empire – Greece, Spain, Sicily and France. Many are still standing. They are just one of the remarkable achievements of Roman engineers.

**A** This is a modern artist's impression of an aqueduct being built.

The discovery of the arch was important. It led to major changes. It allowed the Romans to make great progress in architecture and in the construction of buildings.

**B** This source is taken from the *Concise Dictionary of Greek and Roman Antiquities* (1898).
The first aqueduct was built in 312 BC. Before then the Romans had used the River Tiber and wells sunk in the city. But not enough water could be obtained from these sources and it was unhealthy.

**C** Frontinus described the benefits of the Roman water system in his book *The Aqueducts of Rome*, written in about AD 100. He was the official in charge of aqueducts.
I am concerned with the health and safety of Rome. The results of the great number of reservoirs, fountains and water basins can be seen in people's improved health. The city looks cleaner, and the causes of the unhealthy air which gave Rome a bad name have been removed.

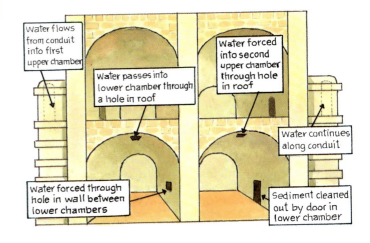

**E** The reservoir of an aqueduct. It helped to remove sediment in the water.

1 a) Look at source A. Describe the various jobs that went into the building of an aqueduct.
b) Does this source suggest the Romans had good safety standards or not?

2 Below is a list of engineering problems that the Romans faced when building aqueducts. Complete the table in your book by listing the solutions found by their engineers.

| Problem | Solution |
|---|---|
| Water carried sediment | |
| Water had to be kept moving | |
| Water must not evaporate | |
| Water must not leak | |

3 Copy the diagram of the reservoir in source E and show the direction of the water flowing through it.

4 Below are three statements. Copy any statement you agree with and correct any that you disagree with.
(i) By inventing the arch, the Romans could construct bigger buildings.
(ii) If the arch had not been invented Rome would have had no fresh water.
(iii) The arch shape meant that aqueducts could be built across valleys.

5 a) Read source B and source C. According to these writers, what changes did the aqueducts bring about?
b) How could a historian find out if these changes actually happened?

**D** The aqueduct at Nîmes in southern France.

# PUBLIC BATHS AND TOILETS

Huge supplies of water were needed to fill the public baths. Here Romans spent much of their free time. The first baths were built during the Republic as places where people could wash. Later they were built by emperors on a much grander scale. Inside there were marble pillars, mosaics and decorated walls.

They were places to meet people, to lounge or swim in one of several pools. Each one was heated to a different temperature by hypocausts.

People could relax in heated rooms, sweating the dirt out of their pores. Then they scraped their skin clean with a strigil. This was a wooden or metal scraper. Those who could afford it then paid masseurs to rub oil into their skin.

Emperors wanted as many people as possible to use the baths. During the Empire there were over a thousand baths in Rome. Admission prices were kept down and children got in free. The baths encouraged people to keep clean. This was important. The Romans believed it helped people to avoid disease.

However, the baths were not only places to wash and swim. They included sports halls where people could take part in wrestling, athletics or other games. Again this was deliberate. The Romans believed that regular exercise kept people fit and healthy. This reduced the risk of disease.

**A** This is a ground plan of the baths of Caracalla. They were built in Rome in the third century AD. At the centre were the baths themselves – a *frigidarium* (cold bath)(5), several tepidaria (warm baths)(6), and a *calidarium* (steam

**B** The remains of a Roman building in Ostia.

**C** This source is taken from *Roman Medicine* by John Scarborough (1969).
The Romans felt the gods were rulers of all things. Everything that happened was controlled by their wisdom and power. They believed that diseases were a sign of the gods' anger.

bath)(7). Most bathers passed through them in that order. There were *gymnasia* on either side of the baths. In addition, there was a sports stadium, with two libraries next to it, and a row of shops and offices.

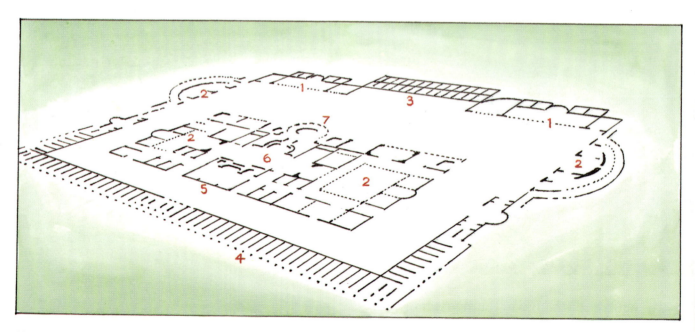

**D** This is a modern artist's impression of toilets at the Roman fort of Housesteads.

**E** The Roman writer Vegetius wrote this account in the fourth century AD.

I will now give some ideas about how the health of the army can be maintained. Regarding the location of army camps, soldiers must not remain for too long near unhealthy marshes, and must not drink from swamps. They should not begin to march too late in the day. They could catch disease due to the sun's heat or the tiredness that would result from the journey.

Daily exercise is far better for the health of soldiers than doctors. If soldiers stay in one place for too long in the summer or autumn, their water supply is polluted and they are made miserable by the smell of their own `excrement`. The air is made unhealthy and causes disease.

**F** The Roman writer Cato made this plea in about 160 BC.

Father Mars I plead with you to take away disease. I beg you to give health to me, my house and my household.

---

**1 a)** Make a sketch of the ground plan of the baths of Caracalla shown in source A.
**b)** Label your plan using the list of buildings below (the list is not in the correct order):
(i) shops and offices; (ii) tepidarium; (iii) frigidarium; (iv) gymnasia; (v) libraries; (vi) calidarium; (vii) sports stadium.
**c)** What evidence suggests that the baths of Caracalla were not just built for exercise?
**d)** How do historians know what these buildings were used for?

**2 a)** What do you think the building in source B was used for?
**b)** What evidence in the photograph leads you to think this?
**c)** Compare source B with source D. What additional information do you learn about Roman toilets from source D?

**3 a)** What do the sources in this chapter tell you about Roman ideas on the causes of disease? Quote from the sources in your answer.
**b)** What would a modern doctor think about these ideas?
**c)** Explain why the views of a modern doctor might be different from a doctor in Roman times.

# 17 ROME AND ITS PROVINCES

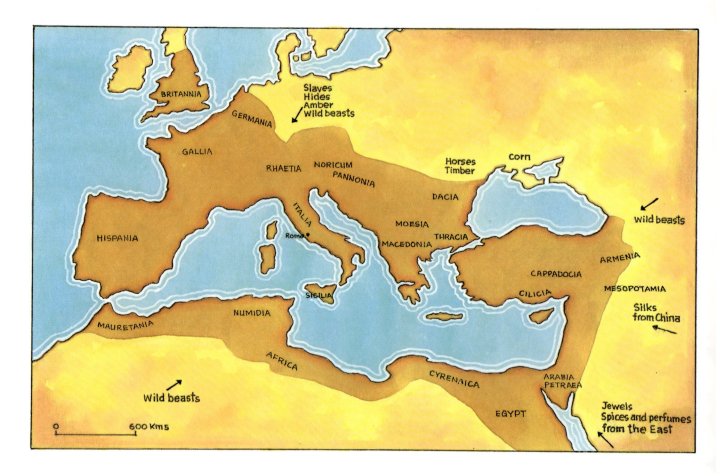

**A** This map shows Roman trade in the first century AD.

Any Roman leader faced two important problems: how to feed the people of Rome and how to pay for the army. The answer was always the same – take food from the provinces and tax the people living there.

The Romans fixed the taxes, but they did not always collect them. Instead they allowed companies of tax farmers to do this on their behalf. At an auction, companies made bids. The company which made the highest bid won the right to collect taxes. Companies were willing to pay a fortune to win it.

However, in order to make a profit, tax farmers had to collect as much money as they could. The Romans took a set amount. Tax farmers took the rest. They sold the houses and possessions of people who could not afford to pay.

Many provincial governors were honest. But there was always the temptation to take bribes. They judged criminals in court cases. For the right price some governors would fix the verdict. Many tax farmers who broke the law also went unpunished.

By the second century AD trade routes connected Rome to all provinces in the Empire. Spanish mines exported gold, silver and copper to Rome. Gaul sent goods made of glass, pottery and tin. From Britain, Rome imported leather and wool.

Three provinces provided wine, olive oil and dried fruit – Greece, Spain and Palestine. These goods were carried in large pots called *amphorae*. Each one was printed with the name of the province it had come from and the date. At Ostia, traders poured the wine and olive oil into their own pots ready to sell. The *amphorae* were not used again, so they were smashed up. Archaeologists have excavated a small hill at Ostia. Most of it is made up of broken pottery from *amphorae*. From these pieces, archaeologists can tell how Rome's imports changed over the years.

**B** This is a model of the London docks built on the River Thames in the first century AD.

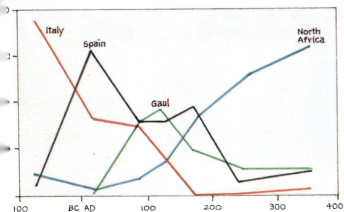

**C** An estimate of the amount of wine and olive oil that was exported to Rome from Italy, Spain, Gaul and North Africa from 60 BC–AD 350.

**D** This source was published in the 'Journal of Economic and Business History', 1928/29. It was translated by M Rostovtzeff from a letter written in Roman times.

Recently a new tax collector was appointed among us. Men who were supposed to owe taxes fled because they were so poor. They were frightened that the tax collector would punish them unbearably. By force, he took their wives, their children, their parents and all the rest of their families.

He hit them and insulted them. He tried to make them say where the men had gone, or else pay their debt. But they did not know and they were just as poor as the men who had run away.

Nevertheless, the tax collector did not release these people until he had tortured them. Others, fearing the same fate, killed themselves by poison, sword or hanging. They thought themselves lucky to be able to die without torture.

1. a) Compare source B with a scene at a modern port. Make a list of the differences that you notice.
   b) What evidence would the maker have needed to produce this model?
2. Look at source C and read the statements below. Then write out the statements you agree with and correct those you disagree with.
   (i) Italy produced the same percentages of wine and olive oil throughout the Empire;
   (ii) During the Republic, North Africa provided only a small percentage of Rome's wine and olive oil;
   (iii) Gaul provided Rome with the most wine and olive oil;
   (iv) Spain was an important producer at the start of the Empire.
   (v) North Africa was the least important producer of wine and olive oil.
3. a) Before you could trust source D, what questions would you want to ask about it?
   b) Why is it important for an historian to ask these questions?

# 18 SLAVERY

When Augustus was Emperor (27 BC–AD 14) about a million people lived in Rome. Historians think that about 300,000 were slaves. They were usually prisoners captured in war.

These prisoners ended up in the slave markets. Men, women and children were sold off to work in the houses of rich Romans. They made possible the good life which these families enjoyed.

According to Roman law, slaves had no rights. They, like their children, belonged to a master. And he had the power of life and death over them.

Many slaves were cruelly treated. The Romans had reason to fear them. Several times during the Republic, slaves revolted against their conditions. Hundreds of slave owners were murdered. Three of the revolts led to wars.

In 132 BC, 70,000 slaves fought the Roman army in Sicily. The revolt was eventually stopped, but a second broke out in 104 BC. This one lasted four years.

More serious still was the revolt of Spartacus. Between 73 and 71 BC his army of gladiators terrorised the whole of Italy. The Republic was in real danger. Ten legions were eventually needed to defeat Spartacus. More than 10,000 slaves were killed in the fighting. Six thousand were captured and crucified along the Appian Way.

**A** Slaves were often forced to fight as gladiators, as shown in this mosaic which was made in about the third century AD.

However, all slaves still had the hope of manumission – freedom from slavery. It was in a master's power to free his slaves. Many did as a reward for good service. Meanwhile, the Senate passed laws which gradually improved the treatment of slaves. Some even worked for the emperors as their advisers. For all this, they were still slaves. As long as the Roman Empire existed, so did slavery.

**B** Thousands of slaves were needed to farm the *latifundia* – the huge slave estates. This is a modern artist's impression of slaves at work. It is based on a bronze medal found at Piercebridge, County Durham. The model was made between the second and third centuries AD.

**C** This source is taken from *Everyday Life in Ancient Rome* by F R Cowell (1961).

The results of slavery could be seen in the way of life of very rich Romans. But slavery also affected the lives of ordinary people. Thousands of Romans could have earned a living by making shoes, clothes, furniture and all the thousands of things used by rich Romans. But they had fewer opportunities to do so. All these things were made by the slaves in the houses of the rich. In addition, slaves were so cheap and plentiful there was no need to invent machinery. The Romans failed to make progress in industry and technology. This was partly due to the reliance on slave labour.

**E** In this source, written in about 40 BC, the Greek writer Diodorus describes the Slave War in Sicily in 132 BC.

Never had there been such an uprising of slaves as now occurred in Sicily. This is what caused it.

The Sicilians had become very rich and bought up large numbers of slaves. They branded them with marks on their bodies. The slaves were so weighed down by the grinding work, beatings and ill-treatment that they could not stand it any longer.

Four hundred slaves led by Eunus – a kind of magician, and conjuror, burst into the city of Enna. They took babies from their mothers' arms and smashed them on the ground. They were joined by a large crowd of slaves in the city. First they killed their masters, then they turned to murdering others.

**D** A rich woman is attended by three slaves. This modern artist's impression is based on a sculpture found in Germany and carved in the third century AD.

Historians have to explain changes that took place in the past. They divide them into two kinds – changes that people meant to happen, and changes they did not plan for. Slavery led to changes in the way Romans lived. Not all of the changes were planned.

1 Look at sources A, B, and D. Write a short paragraph to describe the work being done by slaves in these sources.

2 a) Read source E. According to Diodorus, what caused the Slave War of 132 BC?
b) What is his attitude to the slaves?
c) Suggest reasons why his evidence might be unreliable.

3 a) With a partner look at all the sources again. They all suggest changes in the Roman way of life caused by slavery. Write down each change and say whether it was planned or not.
b) For each change, explain whether it benefited the Romans or not.

# 19 CHRISTIANITY AND THE EMPEROR CONSTANTINE

Jesus Christ was crucified in Jerusalem. Historians are not certain when this happened, but many think he was killed around AD 30. The order for his execution was given by Pontius Pilate. He was the Roman governor of Judea. According to Pilate, Jesus was a criminal who had encouraged people to disobey the Romans.

Jesus' followers thought he was the son of God. They preached his message in Judea and beyond. Soon, thousands of people had become Christians.

Christ's message was special. He talked of love and understanding. He said people should live in peace and always think of others. Their reward would be a life in heaven when they died.

This message was a great comfort to poor people and slaves. They had very little to look forward to. Christianity promised them happiness in the future. No other religion had done this. As a result, many people lost interest in Roman religion.

For years the Romans had allowed people across the Empire to follow their own religions. Eventually, most of these became part of the Roman religion. Christianity did not.

Christians believed in one God. Therefore they did not believe the Emperor was a god. But under Roman law everyone had to pray to the Emperor. Christians refused to do this.

For the Romans this was a serious threat. By breaking the law, Christians had set a bad example to people everywhere. They had to be punished.

During the first and second centuries AD, Christians were persecuted. They could expect a horrible death if they did not worship the Emperor. Many were torn to pieces in wild animal fights, or burnt alive.

Despite this terrible treatment, more and more people became Christians. Finally, in AD 313, the Emperor Constantine changed the laws. People were free to worship whatever religion they chose. Constantine himself became a Christian. He ordered churches to be built in every province.

The Romans had started by attacking Christianity, then become Christians themselves. By the end of the fourth century, Christianity was the official religion of the Empire. Much had changed but Christian beliefs had not.

**A** This tenth-century painting shows the death of Ignatius, Bishop of Antioch.

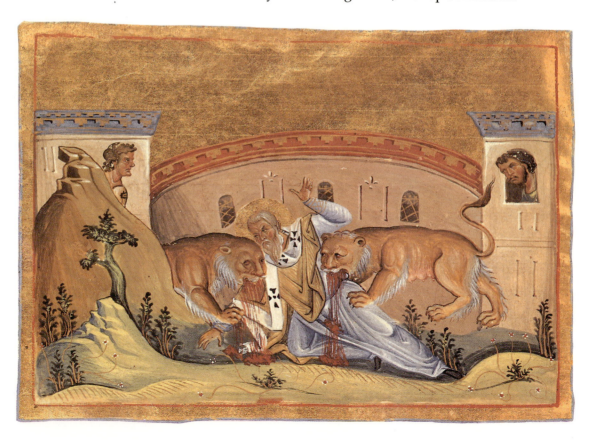

**B** This account is by the Roman writer, Celsus. He wrote in about AD 170.

The Christians speak like this. 'Let no one join us who is educated, wise and sensible. For we think these abilities are evil. But as for anyone who is uneducated or a child, let them join.' The fact is that Christians say these people are worthy of their God. They want them because they are the only people they can persuade – the foolish, dishonourable and stupid, and only slaves, women and children.

**C** This account is taken from *Roman Mythology* by Stewart Perowne (1969).

By the end of the first century, Christianity had many followers in Rome and throughout the Empire. But it is a mistake to think that *all* its followers were poor. Most of them were, it is true, and for this reason. The majority of people in the Empire were poor. Nevertheless, from the beginning, Christianity attracted important men and women. Amongst them was Publius, the Chief Citizen of Malta, and Sergius Paulus, Governor of Cyprus. These were only the first of many educated and intelligent people who became Christians.

**D** This was part of an order given by the Emperor Galerius in AD 311.

The Christians were so obstinate and foolish that they started to make their own laws. When we ordered them to return to the old religion, many were faced with danger and death. Thousands continued with their beliefs and refused to worship or respect our gods. But it has always been our practice to forgive all men.

We will allow these people to be Christians once more. They can attend their churches on condition that they do not upset public order. Because of our goodwill, they are bound to pray to their own God for the safety of Rome. The state will be safe and the Christians will be allowed to live peacefully.

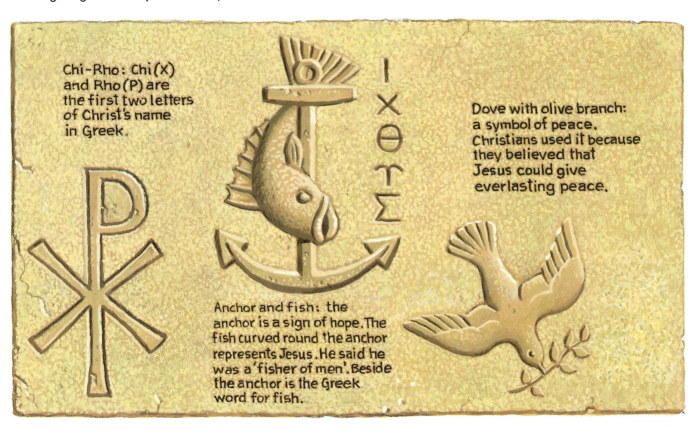

**E** Early Christian symbols. Christians used these signs as a way of recognising each other.

1. a) Compare source B with source C. Explain how these sources give a different impression of the Christians.
   b) Suggest reasons why source C might provide more accurate evidence about the people who became Christians than source B.
2. a) Read source D. Do you think the Emperor Galerius was a Christian or not? Give reasons for your answer.
   b) Why do you think he gave this order?
3. a) Look at source A. Compare it to the position of Christianity at the end of the fourth century AD. What changes had taken place?
   b) Why had these changes happened?
   c) Having read this chapter, write down an example of something that did not change.

51

# 20 ROMAN ARCHITECTURE

One of the Romans' greatest achievements was in architecture. Even today architects throughout the world try to copy their buildings. They design them in what is called the 'classical style'. Buildings in this style are easy to spot. One of the things that makes them different is the use of columns.

The Egyptians invented the stone column. The Greeks developed it. They used rows of marble columns to support the roofs of their temples. The Romans also did this at first.

Later they invented new types of roof and new ways to hold them up. Roman architects still included columns in their designs, but they were not used to support heavy weights as before. The columns were there to make a building look attractive.

Until the third century AD Roman buildings had been made from stone or brick joined with mortar. They experimented with lime and pozzolana – a type of volcanic sand. By mixing this with stone chippings and mortar they discovered an entirely new type of building material – concrete.

This was a major breakthrough. Architects could now design the most spectacular buildings on earth. What made them so strong was their use of arches. These were held in place with concrete pillars. It meant that enormous weights could be supported with ease.

The Romans invented the amphitheatre. They got the idea from Greek theatres which were designed in a semi-circle. The two semi-circles, when joined together, made a circular theatre. It was an entirely new idea. The Romans made the Colosseum possible by using arches – just as they had done to build their bridges and aqueducts.

By experimenting with arches, Roman architects developed a new shape for their roofs – the dome. The best example of this is the Pantheon in Rome. Its domed roof is 43 metres high and made from six layers of concrete. The Pantheon was, and still is, lit by the opening or 'eye' in the roof. It was built between AD 118 and 128 for the Emperor Hadrian.

Roman architects created enormous space inside their buildings. This had never been done before. They developed the column and added to it arches, vaults and domes. Together these make up the classical style of architecture.

**A** This is a scene from a film, *The Fall of the Roman Empire*. It gives us an impression of what Rome might have looked like.

**B** The Roman Forum today. The Temple of Vesta is on the left. On the right is the Temple of Castor and Pollux.

**D** The Colosseum in Rome. It was the largest amphitheatre in the world. It had seventy-six entrances and could hold 50,000 people.

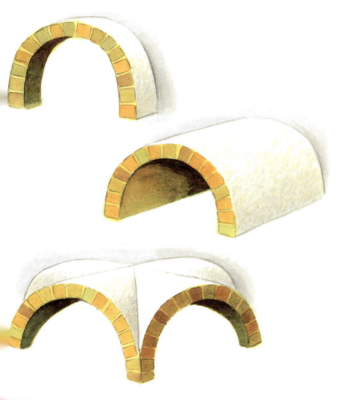

**E** Inside the Pantheon – it was made into a Catholic Church in AD 609.

**C** Three examples of Roman architecture.

1 The Romans built arches with wedge-shaped blocks of stone set in a timber frame. Pillars on either side pressed the wedges together. This gave the arch added strength. Liquid concrete was poured over the frame and allowed to set.
2 By making bigger frames Roman builders could spread concrete over a great distance. This allowed them to construct the tunnel vault.
3 They invented the groyne vault so that two semi-circular vaults could cross each other at right angles. Under the vaults large windows let in light without weakening the walls.

1 'We know what Rome looked like. We've got pictures to show us. So what's the point of keeping a lot of ruins? They may as well knock them down and build something useful like a hospital or a shopping centre.' Do you agree or disagree with this statement? Give reasons for your answer.
2 Look at all the sources in this chapter.
a) Make a list of all the building materials the Romans could use in their buildings.
b) Make a list of all the materials they would *not* be able to use.
3 Look at source E. How was the Pantheon lit? (More than one answer is possible.)
4 Work with a partner. How would you describe the 'classical style' to someone who knew nothing about architecture? Use any of the sources to help you.

# AFTER THE ROMANS

The Romans discovered how to make concrete. They also made use of many different materials in their building: brick, stone, glass, tiles and timber as well as concrete. They built vaults and domes. These were important changes. Because of them the Romans made great progress in architecture.

> But changes do not always lead to progress. Historians sometimes study changes to explain why progress did *not* take place.

You can see this by studying how architecture in Britain changed after the Romans. The Roman Empire ended in about AD 550. Yet 500 years later buildings in Britain were not as good as anything the Romans had built. Many of the skills of the Roman builders were lost and forgotten in Western Europe.

**B** Saxon church at Greenstead, Essex built in about AD 850. This church has been altered considerably since it was first built.

**A** The Arch of Constantine, Rome, built between AD 313 and 315.

**C** Norman church at Barfreston, Kent. The rounded arches on windows and doors are typical of the Norman style of building.

Britain was invaded soon after the Romans left – firstly by the Angles and Saxons, and then by the Vikings. Over the years these tribes forgot their differences and made Britain their home. Meanwhile Roman buildings fell down. There was no one with the skills to repair them. The Britons preferred to live in wooden huts. Wood was the building material they were used to. The knowledge of how to make and use concrete was lost in Britain and Europe for hundreds of years.

In 1066 the Normans invaded Britain. Like the Britons, they did not repair Roman buildings. From the remains it was difficult to work out how they had been built. There were no books to tell the Normans!

At first, most towns were still little more than large villages. Houses were generally built of wood. Roads and streets were made from trampled earth and their towns did not have piped water.

Gradually Norman architects designed better churches. They faced building problems that the Romans had solved a thousand years before. Eventually they built marvellous cathedrals in Britain and France.

D  Ely Cathedral in Cambridgeshire, finished in the thirteenth century.

Historians call the fifteenth and sixteenth centuries the  Renaissance . It was a time of great change in Europe; writers, painters and architects looked again at the achievements of the ancient Greeks and Romans. In Italy especially, architects designed new buildings in the 'classical style'.

At first this did not happen in Britain. King Henry VIII argued with the  Pope  and in 1534 he made himself Head of the Church in Britain.

E  Monument in the garden of Audley End House, near Saffron Walden, Essex. It was built in 1790.

For many years Britain ignored the ideas of the Renaissance. If the ideas came from Catholic countries people thought they could not be good ones! This was unfortunate. Because of the Renaissance, great progress was being made right across Europe – in science, in painting and particularly in architecture.

Britain had to wait until the second half of the seventeenth century. Only then did people really follow the ideas of the Renaissance. Only then did British architects begin to follow the 'classical style'. And they have continued to do so ever since.

F  This house was built in the 1980s.

1  Look at source B and source C. Compare these churches with the Pantheon (source E, page 53). Make a list of the differences you can see.

2  The following sentences may be true or false. Work in groups and write out any true ones and correct any false ones.
   (i) Twentieth century architects do not design buildings in the classical style.
   (ii) Renaissance architects copied the examples of Ancient Greek and Roman architects.
   (iii) The Saxon invasion of Britain led to great progress in architecture.
   (iv) No progress has been made in architecture since the Romans.
   (v) The Norman invasion led to progress in British architecture.

3  a) What type of buildings do you think should be designed in the classical style? Explain why you think this.
   b) What types of buildings do you think would not be suited to this style? Explain your answer.

# 21 THE LATIN LANGUAGE AND ITS INFLUENCE

**A** This wall painting shows a Roman woman, about 50 BC. She is holding a stylus and wax writing tablet.

During the fourth century AD, about 60 million people lived in the Roman Empire. All the different races of people thought of themselves as Roman. What helped bring them together was their common language – Latin.

People in each province still spoke their own language and dialects. But Latin was used for all government business and communication between the provinces.

Few people could read or write. They learnt Latin by hearing it spoken, perhaps at first by soldiers. They heard new words and tried them in their own speech. The vulgar Latin which they spoke was very different to the Latin used by educated people. But this form of Latin lasted longer than the Empire itself. It forms the basis of the Romance languages in Europe today.

Latin was also the official language of the Christian Church, during and after the period of Empire. A thousand years later, all church services were still in Latin. Even today, in many parts of Europe, Latin is still used by the Roman Catholic Church. And any speech or decision made by its leader, the Pope, is always translated into Latin.

**B** The Latin language forms the basis of many European languages, including Italian, French, Spanish and Romanian. English is based on dialects spoken by later invaders but over half its words come from Latin.

| Latin | English | Italian | French | Spanish |
|---|---|---|---|---|
| lex | law | legge | loi | ley |
| civis | citizen | cittadino | citoyen | ciudadano |
| nox | night | notte | nuit | noche |
| turris | tower | torre | tour | torre |

The Romans introduced writing to the provinces of northern Europe and here the Roman alphabet is still used. Originally, this had only 22 letters. The letter *G* was added in the first Century BC; *J*, *U* and *W* appeared during the Middle Ages.

Many English words have been taken straight from Latin. Circus, exit and junior are just a few examples. The English language uses Latin prefixes and suffixes. These are parts added at the beginning of words (prefixes) or at the end (suffixes). By using them, new words can be made.

Mis (meaning badly) is an example of a Latin prefix. It appears in the words misbehave or misunderstand. -ary is a Latin suffix and is used to make primary, dictionary and January.

**C** This is the inscription on the base of Trajan's Column in Rome. It is a good example of Roman capital letters. Over the years printers have copied Roman capitals to make a particular style of printing. We call it the Roman style.

It is through Latin that Greek words have entered the English language. In Europe, during the Renaissance of the fifteenth and sixteenth centuries, there was renewed interest in the ideas of ancient Greece and Rome. Greek books were translated into Latin and because of this we now have words like drama and rhythm.

In the fifteenth century Latin was still the one language known to all educated people. All university lectures were in Latin; so were most of the books that students read. This meant that people from different countries could easily swap ideas.

All plants and animals belong to a particular group or class and have Latin names. Homo sapiens is Latin for wise man. So human beings are classed as the most important animal. This was the idea of the Swedish scientist Linnaeus, who lived in the eighteenth century. Even that long after the Roman Empire, many scientists thought that using Latin was the easiest way to explain their ideas.

In England grammar schools were set up especially for the teaching of Latin. Pupils studied Roman literature. They would hear poems by Juvenal, Horace and Ovid, and be expected to learn them by heart. Above all, they would study the poetry of Virgil. Virgil wrote poetry during the time of Emperor Augustus. He wrote about the old Roman virtues and praised the new Empire set up by Augustus.

Much of Rome's early literature was based on the work of Greek writers. At first Roman theatres only put on Greek comedies and tragedies (serious plays). But during the second century Terence and Plautus began to produce Roman plays. Indeed, William Shakespeare's *A Comedy of Errors* is based on a play by Plautus.

During the Renaissance all these great works of literature were rediscovered. Roman writers have had a great influence ever since, right around the world.

**E** This mosaic from Pompeii shows actors rehearsing for a play.

**F** Masks, like this one, were worn by Roman actors.

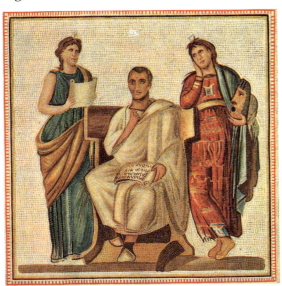

**D** This third-century mosaic from Tunisia shows the Roman poet Virgil (seated). Until his death in 19BC, he worked for fifteen years on *The Aeneid* – one of the most famous poems ever written. It is a long story in verse, and describes the adventures of the legendary Roman hero Aeneas. It also predicts the future greatness of Rome.

1. a) Sub- is another Latin prefix meaning under. Use a dictionary and write out 5 words which begin with this prefix.
   b) -ity is a Latin suffix. Write out 5 words which end with this suffix.
   c) Write down some other Latin prefixes and suffixes that you find in the dictionary.
2. Why did Latin continue to be written and spoken after the end of the Roman Empire? Answer in detail.
3. Please work in groups. Some schools still teach Latin today. Write down arguments for and against this. Afterwards, present your ideas to the class.

# 22  THE EMPIRE'S DECLINE AND FALL

In AD 300 the Roman Empire was still very powerful, and still feared by its enemies. It had a population of over 60 million people. Its borders stretched for 6000 miles across Europe, Asia and North Africa. Despite this, the Empire was in trouble.

For years, emperors had struggled to solve serious problems. They were much worse in the fourth and fifth centuries. This was the period of decline – the time when Rome's power gradually became weaker.

The picture below shows how the design of Rome's border forts changed. In the second century, soldiers marched out to attack enemies in the surrounding area. They were not expected to fight from behind their fortress walls. By the end of the fourth century, small groups of soldiers tried to defend much stronger hill-top forts.

Until the third century, the Empire had steadily increased in size. Each new province meant huge profits for the Romans. But now it had reached its limit. There were no more new provinces – and less money for the Empire. The Romans had to fight costly wars just to keep the lands they had won.

Emperors had less control over the army. They had to bribe their generals and soldiers to stay in power. Emperors who did not pay up were murdered.

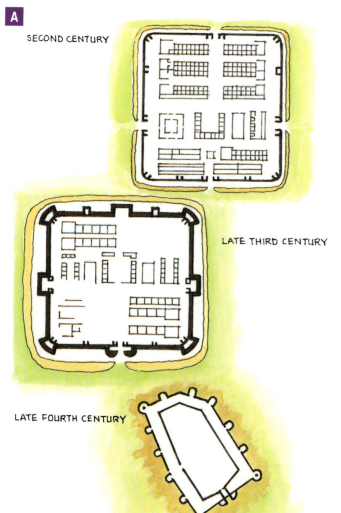

A

SECOND CENTURY

LATE THIRD CENTURY

LATE FOURTH CENTURY

Taxes went up to pay for the army. Higher taxes meant people had less money to spend.

In the towns, traders went out of business. People were unemployed. They had less money to pay taxes.

People moved to the country hoping to find work on villas. The owners needed fewer workers. They grew less crops. People in the towns could not afford to buy them.

The army itself had problems. During the third and fourth centuries AD, it was weakened by civil war. Rival generals fought each other to become emperor. Thousands of soldiers were killed and the borders were left undefended. Barbarian tribes in the north took advantage of this and attacked deep inside the Empire. These tribes had no settled place to live and wanted land from the Romans. They hoped for a better life inside the Empire.

In AD 251 the Goths invaded Moesia. This was a Roman province south of the Danube River. They invaded Greece and marched into Asia. At the same time, the Persian army attacked in the east (see map on page 60).

Emperors were forced to make drastic changes. In AD 285 Diocletian split the Empire in two. He ruled the eastern half and appointed a second emperor, Maximian, to rule in the west. Both emperors needed an army. So 300,000 extra soldiers had to be recruited. Taxes went up again.

The army was always well fed. But everyone else had to put up with food shortages. Thousands of people died from famine and disease. Those who were left wondered if the Empire was worth saving.

*Emperor Constantine built strong forts along the borders. But he moved most of the army to the centre of the Empire. This encouraged the tribes to attack the borders even more.*

*Constantine's army had to be able to move quickly. He reduced the number of footsoldiers and increased the* cavalry *. This upset the legions. They stopped training as hard and lost some of their discipline.*

**B** This source was written by Dio Cassius in about AD 220. From the third century AD emperors paid bribes to barbarian tribes which promised to stop attacking the Empire.

The Emperor Caracalla (AD 211 – 217) fought a war against the Cennians, a German tribe. These warriors attacked the Romans very fiercely. Nevertheless, in return for a large sum of money, the Cinnians let Caracalla say he had beaten them. They also allowed him to escape back into the province of Germany.

Many other tribes asked for his friendship. But their real purpose was to get money. This was made clear by the fact that when he had done as they wished many tribes attacked him. They threatened to make war so Caracalla gave them silver and gold.

**C** Thousands of Roman soldiers were killed in civil wars. So, from the third century, the Romans allowed barbarians to join the army. Their job was to protect the Empire's borders against attack from other barbarian tribes. This source is from *Historia Augusta*, written by an anonymous Roman writer at the end of the fourth century AD.

The Emperor Probus (AD 276 – 82) took 16,000 German recruits into the army. He put them in groups of fifty or sixty with the other soldiers along the border. He allowed 100,000 tribespeople to live in Thrace, a Roman province. They were loyal to Rome. He brought over many people from other tribes – amongst them, the Gepedians and Vandals. But they all broke their promise. When Probus was busy fighting other wars, they roamed about doing a lot of damage to the Romans.

1. a) Look at source A. What changes took place in the design of Rome's border forts?
   b) Why were these changes made?
2. a) Read source B. How did Caracalla deal with the German tribes?
   b) What did he expect to achieve by doing this?
   c) What was the unintended consequence of his decision?
3. a) Read source C. Why did Emperor Probus recruit German tribes into the Roman army?
   b) What did Probus expect to achieve by doing this?
   c) What was the unintended consequence of his decision?
4. Work with a partner. If you had been Emperor in AD 300 what would you have done to solve the Empire's problems? Explain why you would have done this.

# THE END OF THE EMPIRE

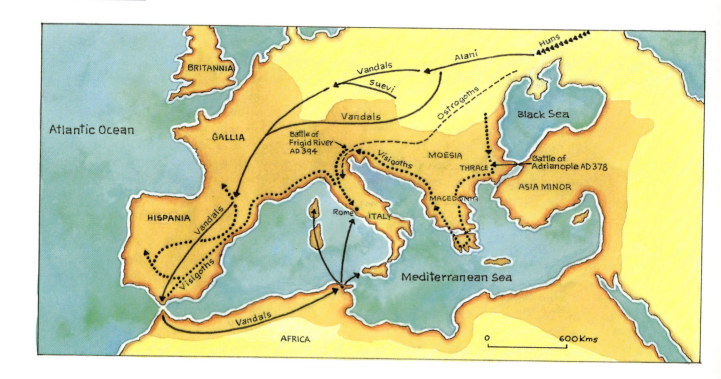

**A** The Barbarian invasions of the Roman Empire.

In AD 376 more tribes crossed into the Empire. Amongst them were the Goths and Visigoths. This time it was not to attack the Romans. They were trying to escape from the Huns. This tribe came from Asia and were now massacring anyone in their way.

The Romans allowed the Visigoths to settle in the eastern half of the Empire. They were starving. The Romans forced them to sell their children as slaves. In return, they received dog meat at the rate of one dog per child.

In AD 378 the tribes got their revenge. The Goths and Visigoths defeated the Romans at the Battle of Adrianople. Forty thousand legionaries were killed or wounded. Not since the days of Hannibal, 500 years before, had a Roman army been so badly beaten.

After the battle, Theodosius, the Roman Emperor in the East, made a deal. He gave the Goths and Visigoths land in Panonia and Moesia. In return, they agreed to fight for the Romans in any future wars.

Meanwhile, civil war again broke out in the Empire. In AD 387 Maximus, a powerful Roman general, led his army into Italy. He wanted to get rid of Valentinian who was Emperor in the West. Theodosius had to come to his rescue. Maximus was defeated, but once again thousands of Roman soldiers were killed fighting each other.

In AD 391 Valentinian was murdered and replaced by Eugenius. Theodosius marched into Italy with an army of 100,000. Twenty thousand of them were Goths led by their king, Alaric. Together, Theodosius and Alaric defeated the army of Eugenius at the Battle of Frigid River.

*More and more barbarians were allowed to join the army. In time, some even became generals. They were far less strict with their soldiers. This set a bad example for the rest of the army. Its discipline got even weaker.*

Alaric expected a reward. When he received nothing from Theodosius, Alaric attacked Thrace and Macedonia. Then he led his army through Gaul and Italy, burning villages and looting towns. In AD 406 the Alans, Suevi and Vandals invaded Gaul. Four years later Alaric captured Rome.

Some of the Empire's problems occurred over a long time. Others happened over a much shorter time. These problems caused the Empire to decline and eventually brought it to an end. Historians explain this change by studying its long-term and short-term causes.

People had got used to the defeats of the army. But Rome had been safe for 800 years. Alaric's attack was a tremendous shock. The Western Empire was all but finished.

Almost, but not quite. In AD 451, the Huns also invaded Gaul. The Roman army joined forces with the Goths, Franks and Burgundians. This combined army defeated the Huns at Chalons in France. It was the last battle that the Western Empire won.

*Eastern emperors did little to help. In Constantinople, their capital city, they continued to pay out huge bribes to the barbarians. They encouraged tribes to attack the West instead of them.*

Now the army was mostly made up of Germans – former tribesmen. In AD 476 they elected Odovacer, one of their commanders, as King of Italy. Emperor Romulus Augustulus was given a pension and told to retire. He left Rome soon after. The Empire in the West was over.

**B** This account of the Huns was written by a Roman writer, Ammianus, in the fourth century.

The Huns lead a more wild life than any other barbarian tribe. They look like men – just – but they are very ugly. Their lives are not  advanced  at all. They do not use fire or any kind of sauce to prepare their food. They eat roots which they find in the fields, and the half-raw meat of any sort of animal. I say half-raw, because they give it a kind of cooking by placing it between their thighs and the backs of their horses.

**C** Vegetius wrote this account early in the fifth century.

Until the death of the Emperor Gratian (AD 375–383) footsoldiers wore breast plates and helmets. But, when they stopped practising on the parade ground, their usual armour began to seem heavy. So they hardly ever wore it. This was because of laziness.

First they asked if they could leave off their breastplates and  chain mail , then the helmets. So our soldiers fought the Goths without any protection for chest and head. They were often killed by arrows. There were many disasters which led to the loss of great cities. But no one tried to make the soldiers wear armour. And so it is, that troops who are wounded think about running and not about fighting.

**D** This new weapon was designed by an anonymous Roman writer, about AD 380. It is taken from the book, *De Rebus Bellicis*.

1  a) Look at source D. How do you think the Romans would use this weapon?
   b) Compare source D with source C. Do you think Vegetius thought this invention would solve the Romans' problems? Give reasons for your answer.

2  a) Read source B. What is Ammianus' attitude to the Huns?
   b) Many Romans shared this writer's views about barbarian tribes like the Huns. Do you think this attitude helped the Romans or not, in their attempts to deal with these tribes? Explain why you think this.

3  Read through this chapter again. In groups, discuss why the Western Empire came to an end. Copy the table below. Fill it in by writing out what you think were the long-term and short-term causes of this great change.

| Long-term causes | Short-term causes |
|---|---|
|  |  |

61

# 23 CHANGE AND CONTINUITY

**A** This sixth-century mosaic shows the Eastern Emperor Justinian with his attendants. In the East people developed Roman ideas, especially in art and architecture.

For years, German tribes had controlled large parts of the Western Empire. Now it was over, they organised their lands into separate kingdoms. This was an important change.

Each tribe had its own king. He ruled everybody in the kingdom, tribespeople and Romans alike. Before, everyone had obeyed the emperor.

From these kingdoms, some of today's European countries developed. The Franks moved into what is now France; the Angles invaded England.

The new German kings were careful not to upset the Romans who remained. At first they allowed the Romans to keep their own laws. Meanwhile the tribes followed German laws which were very different.

Most of the German tribes were no longer barbarian. In Gaul and Italy especially they had learnt to live like their Roman neighbours. They married into each other's families. Soon, it was difficult to tell who were the Romans and who were the Germans.

At first, one important difference between the Romans and the Germans was their language. The Romans spoke Latin. The Germans spoke a variety of different dialects. Gradually people began to speak a mixture of the two. These were called the Romance languages.

This was another major change. But it did not lead to progress. Most people forgot how to speak Latin. They could not read Latin books. Yet these books contained knowledge built up by the Romans over hundreds of years. Now, this was lost.

Despite this, Roman roads were still used centuries after they were first built. And today, across Europe, many railways and motorways follow routes first chosen by Roman surveyors. They connect towns and cities which often date back to Roman times.

Some of these towns started off as army camps, or as walled forts. The Latin word for a walled fort is *castra*. Over the years, *castra* has been changed to '-chester', '-caster' or '-cester'. On modern maps this word is used in many place names.

Not everyone was affected by the end of the Empire. In Britain, many villages had hardly changed since before the Roman invasion. Most Britons still spoke their own Celtic language, worshipped Celtic gods and followed their old customs.

**B** This is the tomb of the German King, Theodoric the Great, in Ravenna, Italy. It was built in AD 526. It shows how at first the Germans borrowed Roman building ideas like the dome and the arch. Later, people in the West forgot how to build them. They had to re-discover this knowledge centuries later.

Much remained the same elsewhere. In the kingdoms, people still worked on large estates as they had done in Roman times. Their new German owners continued to grow crops using the same farming methods.

Like the Romans, most of the German tribes were Christians. So, across Europe, Christianity was still the most important religion. People still built churches. Many were based on the design of the Roman basilica.

Although Rome's Western Empire had ended, the Eastern Empire continued to exist. At various times between the sixth and tenth centuries, it controlled much of Asia and eastern Europe, as well as southern Italy. In these areas it kept alive Roman ideas. In the West, many of these ideas were being slowly forgotten.

One of the most famous eastern emperors was Justinian (AD 527–565). He published a code of all the Roman laws. He believed that all people had equal rights under the law. It did not matter whether they were rich or poor. The law had to treat everyone the same.

Today most countries throughout the world base their own laws on this important idea. Criminals are put on trial. Their cases are heard by a judge and jury. Again, these are words and ideas first thought of by the Romans.

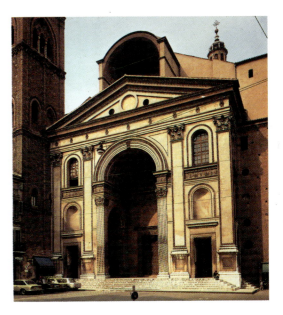

D Roman ideas were important during the Renaissance of the fifteenth and sixteenth centuries. Many architects in France and Italy copied the 'classical style.' This photograph shows the West Front of the San Andrea Church, Mantua, Italy, begun in 1470.

E The Romans piped fresh water to cities and built sewers. It was not until the nineteenth century that European cities had water systems that were as good.

C A page from the seventh-century Lindisfarne Gospels. Latin continued to be the official language of the Church. In monastery libraries monks stored Latin books which described Roman ideas.

1 Work in pairs. Copy and complete this table. On the left, list those things which changed after the Roman Empire. On the right, list those things which did not change.

| Different | Similar |
|---|---|
|  |  |

2 Find a map of Britain. Write down the names of towns and cities which have the words 'chester', 'caster' or 'cester' in them. See how many you can find.

# GLOSSARY

**advanced** – civilised
**advisers** – people who give advice
**allies** – countries which help each other in war
**amphitheatre** – a circular building with seats round an open space
**anonymous** – unknown
**architecture** – the design of buildings
**astronomy** – the study of the stars
**ballistas** – weapons used to throw huge stones
**banquets** – feasts
**barbarian** – an uncivilised foreigner with a different language or customs
**betrayed** – informed on
**booty** – goods stolen from the enemy
**broadside** – the side of a ship between the bows and stern
**campaign** – a series of battles
**Capitol** – the temple of Jupiter
**cavalry** – soldiers on horseback
**chain mail** – armour made from small iron rings linked together
**citizen** – a person given certain rights by the state
**circus** – a building with seats round an open space
**civil war** – a war between people of the same country
**conscript** – force people to join the army
**conspirators** – people who plot to break the law
**crucified** – killed by fastening to a cross
**denarii** – Roman silver coins
**dialect** – how people speak in a particular area
**dictatorship** – a country ruled by one person with all the power
**disband** – break up
**divine** – godly
**entrails** – the insides of an animal
**excrement** – human waste
**exported** – sold to another country
**festivals** – feast days
**garrison** – soldiers who defend a fortress or town
**groma** – an instrument used by Roman surveyors to check the ground was level
**imperator** – commander
**imported** – bought from another country
**imports** – goods bought from another country
**inflammable** – easily set on fire
**inscription** – words carved on stone, or stamped on a coin
**jury** – a group of people who decide if a prisoner is telling the truth
**lease** – an agreement by which landowners allow their land to be used by other people
**legendary** – part of a legend – an ancient story which many people believed
**legion** – a division in the Roman army

**legionaries** – members of a Roman legion
**litter** – a chair or couch shut in by curtains and carried on people's shoulders
**loot** – goods stolen from an enemy
**looting** – stealing goods from an enemy
**lots** – small objects used to decide something by chance
**loyal** – faithful
**lyre** – a small string instrument
**magistrate** – a person who judges cases in court
**massacring** – killing large numbers of people
**masseur** – a person who rubs muscles and joints to make them work better
**mechanic** – a skilled worker
**mercenaries** – soldiers from one country who fight for a different country for money
**monastery** – building where monks or nuns live
**monks** – men who give up their lives to religion and live in a monastery
**mortar** – a mixture of sand, cement and water
**novelties** – things which are new and different
**oath** – a solemn promise
**orators** – public speakers
**overseer** – a person responsible for other workers
**persecuted** – ill-treated
**piers** – pillars used to support an arch
**pivot** – short shaft or pin on which something turns
**plebeian** – a common person
**Pope** – head of the Roman Catholic Church
**province** – land outside Italy ruled by a Roman governor
**quinquereme** – a ship with five rows of oars on each side
**Renaissance** – a rebirth of art and learning in Europe between the 14th and 16th centuries
**reservoir** – a place where water is collected
**revolt** – an uprising by people against a ruler
**sediment** – matter which goes to the bottom of a liquid
**stern** – the back of a ship
**superstitious** – believing in the supernatural
**surveyors** – people who measure and plan roads or check ground is level before building
**tolerant** – willing to let other people have their own opinions or beliefs
**trident** – a three-pronged spear
**trireme** – a ship with three rows of oars on each side
**triumph** – a ceremony to honour a successful Roman general
**volcanic** – produced by a volcano
**vulgar** – common